Time and M
The Journal of
Archaeology,
Consciousness
and Culture

Volume 2—Issue 3—November 2009

Photo: Paul Devereux

Editors

Paul Devereux   John Baker
Neil Mortimer   Michael Winkelman

Managing (and founding) Editors
Neil Mortimer and Paul Devereux

Associate Editors
John Baker
Moorpark College, USA

Michael Winkelman
Arizona State University, USA

Reviews Editor
Jeremy Harte
Ewell Museum, UK

Editorial Advisory Board
Anthony Aveni
Russell Colgate Professor of Astronomy &
Anthropology, Colgate University

Brian Bates
Professor of Psychology, University of Sussex; Visiting
Professor, University of Brighton and Visiting Fellow,
Institute of Professional Studies, University of Sussex

Barbara Bender
Emeritus Professor of Archaeology, Institute of
Archaeology, University College London

Herman Bender
President, Hanwakan Center for Prehistoric
Astronomy, Cosmology and Cultural Landscape
Studies, Wisconsin

Nicole L. Boivin
Leverhulme Centre for Human Evolutionary Studies,
University of Cambridge

David Carmichael
Associate Professor of Anthropology, University of
Texas, El Paso

Christopher Chippindale
Reader in Archaeology & Curator for British
archaeology collections, Cambridge University
Museum of Archaeology & Anthropology; former
editor of *Antiquity*

Timothy Darvill
Professor and Head of Archaeology and Historic
Environment Group, Bournemouth University

Brian Fagan
Emeritus Professor of Anthropology, University of
California, Santa Barbara

Miguel H. Farias
Ian Ramsey Centre, University of Oxford, UK

Dragos Gheorghiu
Professor of Cultural Anthropology and Prehistoric
Ceramics, Department of Postgraduate Studies,
National University of Arts, Bucharest

Martin Gledhill
Architect: Gledhill Walker Associates; University of
Bath School of Architecture

Susan Greenwood
Anthropologist: Visiting Tutor, University of Sussex

Cornelius Holtorf
Associate Professor, School of Human Sciences,
University of Kalmar, Sweden

Ronald Hutton
Professor of History, Department of Historical
Studies, University of Bristol

Bernard Knapp
Professor of Mediterranean Archaeology, University
of Glasgow; editor of *Journal of Mediterranean
Archaeology*

Stanley Krippner
Professor of Psychology, Saybrook Graduate School,
San Francisco

E.C. Krupp
Director, Griffith Observatory, Los Angeles

Charles D. Laughlin
Emeritus Professor of Anthropology and Religion,
Carleton University, Ottawa

Stephen Lekson
Curator of Anthropology, University Museum,
University of Colorado; Editor, *Kiva*

George Nash
Department of Archaeology and Anthropology,
University of Bristol

Timothy R. Paukatet
Professor of Anthropology, University of Illinois

Benny Shanon
Professor of Psychology, The Hebrew University of
Jerusalem

Paul S. C. Taçon
Professor of Anthropology & Prehistory, School of
Arts, Griffith University, Queensland, Australia

Julian Thomas
Professor of Archaeology, School of Arts, Histories &
Cultures, University of Manchester

Christopher Tilley
Professor of Anthropology, Institute of Archaeology,
University College London

Deward E. Walker
Professor of Anthropology, University of Colorado,
Boulder

Robert Wallis
Assistant Professor of Visual Culture/Associate
Director MA Art History, Richmond the American
International University in London

David Whitley
Archaeologist: Adjunct Professor, Department of
Geography, Arizona State University

Aims and Scope
Time & Mind will aim to:

- Provide a dedicated and peer-reviewed forum
  where "cognitive" aspects of archaeology,
  anthropology, and other disciplines can be
  explored and even cross-related where
  appropriate.
- Focus on the sort of papers that hitherto have
  been scattered throughout the peer-review
  archaeological, anthropological and psychological
  literature.
- Publish resource sections within issues for
  academics and practitioners in the field
  on: books recently published; Internet sites;
  developments within the museum world; seminal
  exhibitions, conservation, etc.
- Provide a truly interdisciplinary platform for the
  exchange of ideas and information.
- Become a "cross-over" journal reaching an
  intelligent lay readership beyond its core
  academic audience.

The reach of T&M's content will be global and its
potential range considerable. The full nature of the
journal's remit is left deliberately diffuse—all the
many (and perhaps not yet even fully formulated)
aspects of mind through time will be grist to its mill.

Papers will come primarily from archaeologists,
anthropologists, historians, folklorists and
psychologists, though relevant contributions
from researchers in other fields such as acoustics
(archaeoacoustics), astronomy (archaeoastronomy),
and architecture will also be considered. Where
appropriate and of sufficient quality and significance,
material from non-academically affiliated
contributors will additionally be considered for
peer-review. Contributors will be able to submit
theoretical papers as well as present findings from
specific research projects, provided they address
cognitive aspects. While relevant work in individual
disciplines will be accepted, contributions in which
a cross-disciplinary element predominates will be
encouraged.

Also welcome within the remit of the journal's
content will be submissions exploring how modern
minds—from scholars to "new-agers" and neo-
pagans—project their ways of thinking on to the
past, and also those that present instances where
new findings about the past relate to current
research on the brain and consciousness.

ISSN (print): 1751-696X
ISSN (online): 1751-6978

Berg Publishers is a member of CrossRef

Submissions
To submit an article for consideration, contact the
managing editors at timeandmind@bergpublishers.
com

To submit a book or exhibition review please
contact

Jeremy Harte
Curator
Bourne Hall Museum
Spring Street
Ewell
Surrey
KT17 1UF
UK
Email: Timeandmindreviews@bergpublishers.com

Subscription Information
Three issues per volume. One volume per annum.

2009: Volume 2

Online
www.bergpublishers.com

By Mail
Berg Publishers
c/o Customer Services
Turpin Distribution
Pegasus Drive
Stratton Business Park
Biggleswade
Bedfordshire
SG18 8TQ
UK

By FAX
+ 44 (0)1767 601640

By Telephone
+44 (0)1767 604951

Subscription Rates
Individual print subscription:
(1 year) £25/US$48
(2 year) £45/US$87

Institutional print and online
(1 year) £163/US$317
(2 year) £260/US$508

Online only
(1 year) £138/US$270
(2 year) £221/US$432

Free online subscription for institutional print
subscribers. Full color images available online.
Access your electronic subscription through
www.ingentaconnect.com

Inquiries
Editorial
Julia Hall
jhall@bergpublishers.com

Production
Ken Bruce
kbruce@bergpublishers.com

Advertising and subscriptions
Corina Kapinos
ckapinos@bergpublishers.com

Reprints for Mailing
Copies of individual articles may be obtained from
the publishers at the appropriate fees. Write to:

Berg Publishers
1st Floor, Angel Court
81 St Clements Street
Oxford OX4 1AW
UK

Time & Mind is covered by the following abstracting/
indexing services: Abstracts in Anthropology; BHI
– British Humanities Index; Linguistics and Language
Behaviour Abstracts; Scopus; Sociological Abstracts;
Zetoc

Typeset by JS Typesetting Ltd, Porthcawl, Mid Glamorgan
Printed in the UK

Time and Mind

Volume 2—Issue 3—November 2009

Contents

Articles

Photo: Scott Ashcraft

Book Reviews

Time and Mind:
The Journal of
Archaeology,
Consciousness
and Culture

Volume 2—Issue 3
November 2009
pp. 261–264
DOI:
10.2752/175169609X12464529903056

Reprints available directly
from the publishers

Photocopying permitted by
license only

Editorial

There is an old adage that states you cannot obtain the right answer unless you ask the right question. This is nowhere more true than in archaeological interpretation. The difficulty that can arise is that the cultural worldview the archaeologist operates within can sometimes dampen perception of what the "right" question should be, especially if that question challenges the prevailing mores or if it invokes an area that is currently marginalized. Even if archaeologists manage to sufficiently transcend the discipline's cultural intellectual climate to see what the correct questions are, they may nonetheless feel too inhibited to actually pose them.

This situation has for a long while now affected modern scholarship with regards to the thorny matter of consciousness, still often viewed as a tabooed topic even though in recent decades the steely grip of behaviorism has started to slacken. This unarticulated prohibition infected most academic disciplines to greater or lesser degrees, archaeology included—leaving the ancient mind something of a "black box" in research terms.

Tough Topics

If the climate now is gradually becoming kinder toward open consideration of consciousness, the topic of its close cousin, "non-ordinary" or "altered states of" consciousness, still carries a stigma, often provoking a dismissive attitude, a kind of intellectual yawn, in too much of mainstream scholarship. This can sometimes present a problem for archaeological interpretation because so many premodern cultures *did* seek out non-ordinary mental states in one way or another, through vision quests, resort to environments that promote sensory deprivation, the conducting of ritual practices causing mind-altering mental and physiological stress, and especially the taking of psychoactive substances. As Yulia Ustinova says in her article in this issue, "attaining altered states of consciousness was a socially approved and admired way of arriving at visions." It might not be the case now, but it was then. We have to climb out of our own cultural boxes and personal likes and dislikes and take that fact on board if we wish to fine-tune our interpretations, and that is why T&M encourages papers that explore ancient relationships with non-ordinary mind states and, indeed, other topics that can also suffer from too much modern cultural filtering. (As always, though, this isn't a license for sloppy scholarship.)

Ustinova's discussion in this issue on ancient Greek oracle caves looks at how two forms of mind-altering conditions, sensory deprivation and the presence of noxious gases in some caves, were key to their use. She notes how these facts have been overlooked, resisted, or sidelined, so much so that the *pneuma* at Delphi that supposedly inspired the prophetesses there was actively dismissed by leading scholars as having been a myth until recent geological research rendered such a viewpoint questionable.

Other articles in this issue include Ronald Hutton's fine study comparing the histories of modern druidry and the "Earth Mysteries" movement in Britain, showing the connections and disconnections between them. For those unfamiliar with it, the Earth Mysteries phenomenon involved a popular mix of fringe interests in archaeology that started to meld together in the 1960s onward. Earth Mysteries was never a coherent movement as such, but more a collision of ancient-astronaut ideas, Atlantean and other "golden age" notions, neopaganism, alternative archaeological enthusiasms including "ley hunting," dowsing, and occultism, plus a genuine popular interest in aspects of archaeology such as archaeoastronomy.

While much Earth Mysteries material lacked academic substance, some creditable strands came out of it. For instance, Earth Mysteries enthusiasts were slightly ahead of the curve in appreciating that archaeological sites need to be considered holistically in terms of their landscape environments, that sites should not necessarily be treated

in isolation. What today's archaeology refers to as "phenomenology of landscape" and "sensory archaeology" have their antecedents in Earth Mysteries, however hotly denied. Moreover, some of today's British archaeologists had their initial interest in archaeology roused by Earth Mysteries, though only the brave are prepared to admit to it. And some authentic research strands also emerged from Earth Mysteries. For example, even now many archaeologists fail to see that such a topic as "leys" (or "leylines" as they are typically referred to in New Age literature) was not only deconstructed in its erroneous popular incarnation by some key figures within the later Earth Mysteries "movement" but was used to launch a respectable scholarly study of archaeological and social historical features such as "death roads" in premodern Europe. Many archaeologists still need to update their knowledge of that literature and to separate it out from old and current New Age notions.

A fine and detailed example of a site treated holistically in both spatial and temporal contexts is provided in this issue by Johannes Loubser in his study of Judaculla Rock, a petroglyph boulder in North Carolina's Balsam Mountains. And not forgetting good old-fashioned archaeological debate, we have Lionel Sims arguing that the eighteenth-century antiquarian William Stukeley was probably correct when he described the course and western end point of Beckhampton Avenue, the now lost stone rows that connected with the west side of the great Avebury henge monument in Wiltshire. Yet again, Sims suspects, archaeologists have underestimated the worth of Stukeley's records.

Time and Mind   Volume 2—Issue 3—November 2009, pp. 261–264

This issue also contains its usual stimulating range of book reviews, and of correspondence—which we encourage. Indeed, we welcome comments, viewpoints and well-informed critiques of articles.

Onward

This issue signals the completion of the second year (Volume Two) of this journal's publication, and we wish to thank readers, institutions, and contributors alike for their support, not to mention the goodwill and help from members of our editorial advisory board and the numerous other scholars who have taken time out to conduct reviews of submissions. We should also note that T&M has now been entered on the

SCOPUS index, an international academic yardstick which should give librarians greater confidence in taking out institutional subscriptions to T&M.

We take this opportunity to signal that in the next issue, the first of Volume Three, we will be announcing details of changes to our editorial line-up: nothing too drastic, just necessary adjustments.

It may be the end of our second year of published existence, but we've barely got going with the T&M mission— there is fascinating research and other material yet to explore. (And doubtless debate and controversy too!) We hope you will continue to travel with us on this adventure.

Time and Mind:
The Journal of
Archaeology,
Consciousness
and Culture

Volume 2—Issue 3
November 2009
pp. 265–286

DOI:
10.2752/175169609X12464529903092

Reprints available directly
from the publishers

Cave Experiences and Ancient Greek Oracles

Yulia Ustinova

Yulia Ustinova is an Associate Professor at the Department of
General History, Ben-Gurion University of the Negev, Israel.
Her research focuses on ancient Greek religion and makes
use of a multidisciplinary approach based on the application
of results of neuroscience, anthropology, and sociology to
the interpretation of historical phenomena. Among her
publications are articles on various aspects of religion and
culture in the Mediterranean area, and two books: *The
Supreme Gods of the Bosporan Kingdom: Celestial Aphrodite
and the Most High God* (Brill, 1999) and *Caves and the Ancient
Greek Mind: Descending Underground in the Search for Ultimate
Truth* (Oxford University Press, 2009). yulia@bgu.ac.il

Abstract
A great number of Greek oracular cults focused on caves,
notwithstanding the divergent nature of the divine patrons
of these cults. The fundamental reason for locating
prophetic activities in caves was the need of the gods'
mediums to attain divine inspiration, that is, to alter their
state of consciousness. For the purposes of divination
the Greeks used at least two methods. The easiest and
universally practiced technique was sensory deprivation.
Modern research demonstrates that reduction of external
stimuli leads to dream-like states, involving release of
internal imagery. In the geographic setting of Greece,
caverns and grottos provide an easy way to achieve
total or near-total isolation. The second technique was
based on special geological conditions, namely, a source
of poisonous gas having euphoriant or psychotropic
effect. The psychotropic or, in the opinion of the Greeks,
numinous quality of the caves was common knowledge to
such a degree that the association of seers and prophets
with caves became universal.

Key words: caves, altered states of consciousness,
sensory deprivation, ancient Greece, oracles

Introduction[1]

In contrast to tradition in many other cultures, oracles, and especially oracles directly inspired by the gods, played an extremely important role in ancient Greek religion and culture. The will of the immortals was announced to the mortals either in established sanctuaries, by members of temple personnel, or simply by laymen who believed they were in direct contact with the gods (Vernant 1974; Rosenberger 2001; Burkert 2005).

The sheer number of oracles known to be focused on caves is no less than astonishing. Of the forty centers marked by V. Rosenberger on his map of the important Greek oracles (Rosenberger 2001: 214–15), natural and artificial grottos played a crucial role in the vatic practices of eleven (those at Delphi, Lebadeia, Ptoion, Oropus, Aegira, Bura, Olympia, Lycosoura, Delos, Hierapolis, and Claros). With the addition of less famous oracular grottos, this number increases considerably. Entering caves regularly occurs as a major requirement for a prophetic séance, both in established cults and in the activities of individual seers.

There must be an important reason for locating prophetic activities in caves. I suggest that it was the need of the gods' mediums to attain divine inspiration, that is, to alter their state of consciousness. The quest for the ultimate truth is the kernel of inspired prophecy. For the Greeks, its knowledge belonged to the gods alone, and could not be perceived by the limited human mind, held back by mundane thoughts (Plato, *Phaedo* 66 DE; Snell 1960: 136; Starr 1968: 349, 351). To share in the immortals' knowledge, one had to liberate the soul from the burden of the mortal body by

becoming *entheos*, "having the god inside him- or herself": the seer or prophet served as mediums, conveying superhuman knowledge by means of their bodies. In the grip of the god, the medium could display a wide range of abnormal behavior, from mere detachment and aloofness to violent paroxysms. These mental states, which today would be referred to as "altered states of consciousness" or "non-ordinary consciousness" were *enthousiasmos* (divine possession) or *mania* (madness, frenzy) for the Greeks (Plato *Timaeus* 71 E–72 B; *Phaedrus* 244AB; Delatte 1934: 5; Motte 2004: 247–52; Dodds 1973: 64–101). Whatever was perceived or uttered in these states, prophecy, poetry, or mystical insights, was considered to be inspired by the gods and immeasurably superior to anything deliberated by the senses in sobriety (Cornford 1952: 88–106; Chadwick 1942; Vernant 1974: 12–13; Murray 1981). In modern words, attaining altered states of consciousness was a socially approved and admired way of arriving at visions, which were very different from any thoughts produced by the normal waking consciousness and interpreted encounters with ultimate divine reality.

This article demonstrates that one of the most common techniques of attaining prophetic revelations in Greece was a sojourn in an isolated chamber or grotto. The fundamental reason for the predilection for such places in the quest of divine truth was that they provided an environment where consciousness could be manipulated with least difficulty. The easiest and universally practiced technique was sensory deprivation. The second technique was based on special geological conditions, namely, a source of poisonous gas having euphoriant or psychotropic effect.

Caves and Sensory Deprivation

Caves humble and overwhelm human beings (Devereux 2000: 87–96). His rationality notwithstanding, Seneca succumbed to the numinosity of a huge cavern: "When a cave supports a mountain on rocks deeply eroded from within, not made by human hand, but excavated to such size by natural causes, your soul is seized by a religious apprehension" (*Epistulae* 4.41.3).

Cave experiences are many-sided. Caves are sometimes difficult to get to; entering a cave means crossing the border between the worlds of the familiar and the unknown, a very significant action bringing about discomfort, fear, and even true claustrophobia (Whitehouse 2001; Roux 1999: 320–1). Disorientation and diminished vision, as well as changes in olfactory and auditory perception, make even a short stay in a deep cave very different from the routine experience of most people, notwithstanding their cultural and social diversity. Ridden by fear, people who enter caves even for a short time may lose control of their actions and feelings, just as it happened in the Marabar Caves to the characters of E.M. Foster's *A Passage to India.*

Deep caves are pitch black and almost entirely sound-proof. When modern guides leading cave tours switch off electricity, and the visitors find themselves in absolute darkness, with only the gentle plop of distant drops of water or flutter of bat wings breaking the complete silence, even those with strong nerves grow tense. Now let us imagine a mystic, shaman, or visionary

voluntarily entering a cave, perhaps after a fast, and staying there alone for some time.

In a deep cave, under conditions of almost total suppression of sensory input, our mind enters a state of severe "stimulus hunger," and the subjective self emerges forcefully (Solomon 1965; Zubek 1969; Austin 1998: 102–4; La Barre 1980: 39; Wulff 1997: 76; West 1975: 300; Martindale 1981: 316; Geels 1982: 44; Siikala 1982: 105; Merkur 1985: 172; Joseph 2003: 9). Cavers and geologists who specialize in the study of caves report visual and auditory hallucinations, especially after remaining underground for long periods (Clottes 2004).

When awake, the human mind needs to be occupied permanently. Elimination of external stimuli forces the mind to concentrate within itself, and brings about intensive discharge of inner imagery. This condition is known as sensory deprivation. Normal people participating in laboratory tests, when placed in dark sound-proof spaces, start to hallucinate after a few hours, experience the sensation of floating, or press the "panic button" to be let out (Suedfeld 1969; Kubie 1965; Vernon et al. 1965; Freedman et al. 1965; Martindale 1981: 99, 255; Winkelman 2000: 149; Austin 1998: 102). In an autobiographic account of experiments with solitude-isolation tanks, physician and psychoanalyst J.C. Lilly describes his own "dreamlike states, trancelike states, mystical states," which comprised encounters with celestial teachers and divine guardians (Lilly 1972: 40, 42).

Sensory deprivation is one of the common techniques of inducing altered states of consciousness. They can be attained by different methods, and involve different experiences, but they share a most important common characteristic: they silence the waking consciousness and free the mind from the limitations of the alert ego, allowing self-transcendence and awareness undisturbed by the external world (James 1961: 329; Hood 1997; Ellwood 1980: 15–17; Geels 1982: 28–9; Laski 1990: 41; Hollenback 1996: 40–1; Shanon 2002: 262–3; Austin 1998: 24–30; Gimello 1978: 178; D'Aquili and Newberg 1998: 193–4; Lex 1979: 122–30; Ludwig 1968; Martindale 1981: 316–20; Wulff 1997: 188–99; Winkelman 2000: 148–52; 2002: 1878; 2004: 198; Pearson 2002: 74).

Non-ordinary or altered states of consciousness vary in their intensity, from conditions in which the experiencer remains aware of his environment to deep unconscious states (Siikala 1982; Lewis-Williams 2002: 134; Harner 1990: 48–9; Austin 1998: 21). They are actively sought within many societies (Shanon 2002: 324–6). For example, in ancient Greece, certain forms of madness, considered to be inspired by supernatural forces, were actively sought. "Our greatest blessings come to us by way of madness, provided it is given us by divine gift," says Socrates in Plato's *Phaedrus* (244A; Dodds 1973: 64). In contrast, other kinds of madness were expunged, either by purifications or other religious means, or by more rational methods (Ustinova 1992–8, with refs).

For the experiencer the truth attained in hallucinations is purer than mundane knowledge and immutable (D'Aquili and Newberg 1998: 195; Ellwood 1980: 20; Shanon 2002: 264–6; Streng 1978: 146). Altered states of consciousness create "an enhanced sense of reality," their noetic quality manifests itself in the feelings of

illumination and ultimate salience, and they change the experiencer's attitude to life (Ramachandran and Blakeslee 1998: 180, 185–7; cf. Winkelman 2000: 152; Newberg et al. 2001: 110; Andresen 2001: 268; Shanon 2002: 265). These states involve wordless comprehension and are hence difficult to describe; as a consequence, experiencers and their community often regard them as ineffable (Austin 1998: 515–16; Geels 1982: 52).

Floating in an isolation tank is the most radical way to cut off somatosensory input. However, sensory deprivation does not need to be extreme in order to result in altered states of consciousness. Withdrawal to caves and solitary places is known to lead to the attainment of visions and revelations. Even reductions in information input force the alert mind to start projecting its own contents onto the consciousness: the individual then has vivid fantasies or hallucinates (Hastin Bennet 1965; Shurley 1962; La Barre 1980: 43; Merkur 1985: 172; Wulff 1997: 76.). Lack of external input forces the mind to focus on every minimal stimulus the environment offers. Thus, rare sounds or a spot of light in the dense darkness of a cave may lead to vivid hallucinations (Martindale 1981: 317; Austin 1998: 102).

Mystics and ascetics practicing social isolation in order to achieve enlightenment attained alterations of consciousness by reducing external stimuli: dwelling in a cave, in a hollow tree, in an isolated cell, or at the top of a pillar not only reduced the distractions of the human society, but also caused disturbances in body image and auditory and visual hallucinations (Ludwig 1968: 71; Wulff 1997; Blacker 1975: 50, 53, 63–4; Hollenback 1996: 96–119; Merkur 1993: 30–3; Roux

1999: 300–7; 310–15). Examples from various periods and cultures are abundant.

Social isolation and sensory deprivation are among the most common techniques used by shamans in their deliberate vision quest. Round about puberty, the individual suffering anxiety and/or sensing his shamanic vocation withdraws to a lonely place, such as a cave, den, or hole in the snow, and stays there for several days, fasting. During this vigil the future shaman has a vision, which would guide him for the rest of his life (Merkur 1985: 134, 144, 171–6; Merkur 1993: 31; Winkelman 2002: 1876; Harner 1990: 22; Lewis 1989: 32). D. Lewis-Williams (2002), looking for the origins of the Palaeolithic parietal art, argues convincingly that it was mental imagery of shamanistic trances experienced in the depth of the caves that led the prehistoric painters to image-making in caverns.

Accounts of the rigorous spiritual discipline followed by Celtic seers, before uttering prophecy, include preliminary period of seclusion, special diet, and absence of distraction (Chadwick 1942: 6). Early Buddhists believed that in order to obtain supernatural powers (of invisibility, clairvoyance, traveling through the air, etc.) one had to "bring his thoughts to a state of quiescence, practice diligently the trances, attain to insight, and be a frequenter of lonely places" (Hollenback 1996: 190; 199; Gimello 1978: 180–3). The account of a yogic method of achieving knowledge of *Brachman*, the Absolute in the *Svetasvatara Upanishad*, entails retirement to a solitary place, such as a mountain cave, as a prerequisite for meditation and realization of the truth (Ellwood 1980: 49; Stace 1960: 42). In Senegal, the Wolof *marabouts* still withdraw

into caverns in order to obtain visions (Rouget 1990: 47, 52).

According to the Jewish tradition, encounters of several spiritual leaders with their God took place in caverns. Moses spoke to the Lord in the Meeting Tent, but when he asked to see God's glory, the Lord placed him in a hollow of a rock (Ex. 33.22). Having fled from Jezebel, Elijah the prophet abided in a cave in the wilderness, and heard the voice of God (1 Kings 19.9–18). Jewish apocalyptists combined isolation in nocturnal darkness, fasting, sleep deprivation, and deliberate mood alteration, in order to attain visions and spiritual communion with the divine (Merkur 1989). Rabbi Simeon ben Yohai, miracle worker and sage, spent more than twelve years in a cave together with his son, left it by the god's order, and performed miracles and purifications (*Babylonian Talmud, Tractate Shabbat*, 33B–34A; Rosenfeld 1999). These narratives seem to reflect the popular belief that the withdrawal into a cave was inductive to numinous experiences of hearing or seeing the god.

The most famous revelation ever recorded, the Apocalypse of St. John, is supposed to have been written in a cave on the island of Patmos, where St. John was banished in AD95 (Euseb. *Hist. Eccl.* 3.18.1; 3.20.8–9). The cave, known as the Holy Grotto of Revelation, is now encircled by the monastery of St. John the Theologian. The legend associating the vision of the *Apocalypse* with a cave may have been prompted by the tradition of solitary contemplation as a way to enlightenment, which is attested in later Christianity (Roux 1999: 301–7; McGinn 2005: 243; Stace 1960: 186–96). The contemplative life of Carmelite nuns is based on "stripping away" of all the distractions by living in a bare cell, and by absolute silence (Chadwick 1942: 66–8; Rouget 1990: 44). The Shakers of Saint Vincent (the Antilles) withdraw into "secret rooms" where they undertake their spiritual journeys in isolation and immobility (Rouget 1990: 54). Thus, mystics of assorted denominations seek a "kind of mentally induced anesthesia of corporeal senses" (Hollenback 1996: 170) in order to achieve the state of consciousness leading to mystical experience.

Chemical aspects of sensory deprivation are most revealing. Many hallucinogenic drugs act by impairing sensory input (Iversen 2001: 53). Altered states of consciousness, usually associated with drug consumption, can also be reached without these external aids (Zuckerman 1969: 122). Endorphins, natural opiates in the brain, act as natural euphoriants in the human body, and one of the triggers of endorphin discharge is sensory deprivation (Lewis 1989: 10, 34; Blackmore 1993: 107; Winkelman 2004: 208) Hence, blocking sensory input in any way seems to lead to visions and hallucinations, irrespective of the technique employed, whether drug use or withdrawal to an isolated place.

In neurological terms, there is no consensus on the biochemical and neurophysiological mechanism of hallucination in a state of sensory deprivation (Wulff 1997: 77; D'Aquili and Newberg 1998: 194; Newberg et al. 2001: 40; Lex 1979: 132–47; Newberg and D'Aquili 2000: 56; cf. Andresen 2001: 260–1). Subjective senses of absolute spacelessness and of limitlessness of self are prominent in the descriptions of sensory deprivation. Another subjective result of sensory isolation may be reaching

an out-of-body experience (OBE), known also as ecsomatic state, transport, soul flight, soul journey, or astral projection. Such experiences range from brief, "everyday" sensations of watching oneself from a distance, which can be felt while quite awake, to a deep mystical state (Blackmore 1993; Gabbard and Twemlow 1984: 22–3; Green 1968). Cross-cultural distribution of these experiences suggests that they result from the common neurological characteristics of the human mind.

Thus caves and dark spaces, creating conditions of stimulus hunger or sensory deprivation, can be instrumental in attaining various altered states of consciousness, ranging from intense contemplation to visions, hallucinations, and out-of-body experiences. Haruki Murakami weaves these ideas into the plot of his novel *The Wind-up Bird Chronicle*, making its main character descend into a deep well to live through a breathtaking adventure of hallucinations and visions.

Cave Oracles

To comprehend the reasons which impelled the Greeks to associate inspired divination with caves and grottos, we will now briefly survey textual and archaeological evidence on some oracular shrines and reassess the nature of their cults. Then we will juxtapose this data with observations on the neuropsychology of altered states of consciousness. The resulting insights will provide some keys to the Greek predilection for caves in their quest of divine wisdom.

Oracles of the Nymphs and Pan
Caves were often sacred to the Nymphs, youthful and mischievous residents of

water-springs, rivers, mountains, and groves (Larson 2001). Pan, the god of wild nature, dwelt in caves, and was often worshiped in conjunction with the Nymphs (Borgeaud 1988: 49). Dozens of caves sacred to the Nymphs and to Pan are known today (Amandry 1984: 404–9; Faure 1964: 141–2, 149–50; Edwards 1985: 19–27; Borgeaud 1988: 48–9, 151–4, 207; Lavagne 1988: 60–2; Larson 2001: 226–58; Herter 1937; Brommer 1956: 992–1007). Pan was also able to seize or invade human beings, making them panoleptic, possessed by the god. Panolepsy brings about divine inspiration, which confers mantic abilities. Both panic and panolepsy are numinous, both are indicative of the god's presence, but in different ways (Borgeaud 1988: 103–13). Panic is entirely negative, it paralyses every emotion but fear, while panolepsy, in contrast, like other types of divine possession, is a temporary elevation above the normal human condition. It may be frightening and seem weird, but it inspires hallucinations that have noetic quality. No wonder that in his native Arcadia, Pan was the foremost oracular deity (Borgeaud 1988: 3, 47; Jost 1985: 491). He was credited with the ability to inspire vatic utterings in Attica as well as in Arcadia (Menander *Dyscolus* 571–2; Gomme and Sandbach 1973: 134, 223).

Prophetic inspiration and poetic rapture, as well as other kinds of madness, were ascribed to nympholepsy, possession by the Nymphs (Plato, *Phaedrus* 238CD; Pollux 1.19; Hesychius s.v. *numpholêptoi*; Iamblichus *De mysteriis* 3.10; Pausanias 4.27.4, 9.3.9, 10.12.11; Borgeaud 1988: 106; Connor 1988: 160). In the cave of the Nymphs on Mt. Cithaeron many local inhabitants became nympholepts, possessed and endowed

with oracular powers (Plutarch *Aristides* 11; Pausanias 9.3.9).

A fascinating case of possession by the Nymphs is attested to by inscriptions from the cave at Vari in Attica (Schörner and Goette 2004): in the late fifth–early fourth century BC, Archedamus of Thera, who devoted much time and care to the cave, experienced states of trance there, most probably on numerous occasions, which he describes as "seizure by the Nymphs" (*Inscriptiones Graecae* I³ 977–80). In one of these seizures, as his dedication states, he had a vision of the Nymphs instructing him "to work out" the cave. According to the inscriptions, Archedamus embellished the cave and planted a garden near its entrance. He even carved his self-portraits there: crude low reliefs of a man holding stoneworking tools appear twice near inscriptions mentioning his name. The inner part of the cave is dominated by a rudely cut and mutilated enthroned figure, as well as by an oval object, both hewn out of the rock. These are most probably representations of a Nymph and of an *omphalos*. The *omphalos* is a recognized symbol of the oracular center at Delphi (see below) and designates the prophetic function of Archedamus' cave. *Omphaloi* are found in other prophetic caves, for instance at Claros. It is noteworthy that the oracular god Apollo was worshiped in the cave together with the Nymphs (*Inscriptiones Graecae* I³ 981; Wickens 1986: 2: 115; Farnell 1907: 4: 130; Schörner and Goette 2004: 47–9).

The Vari cave, rich in natural and man-made awe-inspiring features, offers a rare opportunity to contemplate the emotions of a believer, and in particular of a nympholept, inside a cave Nymphaeum. Archedamus returned to the darkness of the cave, lighted by a torch or a lamp, to worship the Nymphs, engrave his dedications, and depict himself on the rock. The intentions behind the extraordinary act of self-portraiture can only be surmised, but it could not been mere mundane self-commemoration. Was it a wish to merge with the walls of the sacred cave? To stay forever together with the Nymphs? To dedicate himself to them? Regrettably, he did not explain.

We can speculate how the altered state of consciousness described by Archedamus as nympholepsy was reached. A stay in the darkness and silence of the cave was perhaps sufficient; if a person entered it with some faint source of light, the powerful figure of the seated Nymph, stalactites, and other natural features could inspire fantastic visions (Connor 1988: 184–9). Mental images passing through the mind during such a sojourn could readily be interpreted as prophetic revelations.

Several other cases of nympholepsy (Larson 2001: 238, 257; Mitford 1980; Masson 1966: 20–1; Masson 1981) attested epigraphically suggest a remarkably constant pattern which includes, first, a cave as the mise-en-scène, second, possession by the Nymphs or at least their cult, and third, endowment of chosen devotees with inspired visions, vatic or poetic abilities (Larson 2001: 18).

The cave itself became in some cases just an emblem of divinely enthused prophecy: in several popular centers of divination (for instance, the Corycian cave), the emphasis shifted from inspired vaticination to lot oracles, which even then retained the patronage of the Nymphs (Amandry 1984; Larson 1995: 347). Many less frequented

caves preserved their reputation as places of nympholepsy or panolepsy.

It is almost self-evident that Pan and the Nymphs, unrefined deities of nature, would be worshiped in the wild, in their pristine abodes. It is also only to be expected that men born and bred to live in human society, when separated from it in an untamed landscape, would feel a spectrum of emotions from fear to bucolic delight, and would ascribe these sensations to the gods of the countryside. No commonsensical explanation can clarify why a stay in a cave supposedly belonging to Pan and the Nymphs would cause people to hallucinate and utter prophecies. However, if the effects of isolation and sensory deprivation are considered, panolepsy and nympholepsy become less mysterious: they ensued from a normal reaction of the human mind to these conditions.

Cave Oracles along the Valley of Meander

Caves, dark and menacing, seemed bottomless to people who did not dare to penetrate their damp depths. Unsurprisingly, they invited the image of the netherworld, were often considered entrances to Hades, and called Charonia or Plutonia, after Charon the ferryman of the dead and Pluto the lord of the netherworld. The idea that caves served as passages to the netherworld was so common that even relatively unimposing grottos could be given the title of Plutonium. Many of these caverns were used for divination.

Oracles of the dead were usually placed at the entrances to the Netherworld. More often than not, these *nekuomanteia* were located in caves: out of the "big four" named by D. Ogden, the oracles at Taenarum and at Heracleia Pontica were based in caves, and the one at Avernus near Cumae was intrinsically associated with caves in myth (Ogden 2001).

The valley of Meander in Asia Minor presents a distinctive type of oracles. Strabo reports the existence of three Charonia along the Meander: at Hierapolis, at Acharaca and the Aornum near Magnesia, and explains the multiplicity of cave oracles by soil conditions, favoring the formation of caves (Strabo 12.8.17; 14.1.11; Ustinova 2002). They were located in caves emitting mephitic gases, deadly or dangerous for ordinary people. For instance, at Hierapolis (modern Pamukkale) there was a deep cave with a narrow opening filled with misty poisonous vapors which killed every animal entering the cave. Only the eunuch priests of the goddess Cybele were able to enter the cave, either due to their techniques of holding their breath, or antidotes, or a phenomenon like *enthousiasmos* (Strabo 13.4.14; Pliny *Historia Naturalis* 2.95; Dio Cassius 68.27.3). The Plutonium has been identified: it is a deep chamber and a hole, emitting highly poisonous gases. Thus, ancient accounts of gas discharge have been verified by modern scientists and found precise (Bean 1989: 202–4, fig. 82; Cross and Aaronson 1988; Negri and Leucci 2006).

A fragment from a treatise by a sixth-century AD Neoplatonist, Damascius, gives a description of a temple of Apollo at Hierapolis, with a descent into the noxious grotto and visions he experienced there, including the promise of escape from Hades (Zintzen 1967: 176).

Excavations of the site revealed a temple of Apollo adjacent to the cavern. There was direct access to the Plutonium from inside the temple of Apollo, and recently geophysical research demonstrated that a fault passed immediately beneath the temple. The existence of a direct connection between the mephitic cavern and the temple of Apollo suggests that Damascius' description is correct: one could enter the grotto from the temple (Bean 1989: 206–7; de Bernardi Ferraro 1993: 138–43; Negri and Leucci 2006). The most probable explanation of this connection would be utilization of the hallucinogenic qualities of the gas, in order to produce (prophetic) visions.

Cave Oracles of Gaia

That Gaia, the goddess of the Earth, would be worshiped near or inside openings leading into the depth of the earth appears as self-evident as the location of Ploutonia and oracles of the dead at such places. The association of divination with the goddess of the earth seems to be very ancient (Bouché-Leclercq 1879–82: 2, 251–60). In several cases, Gaia's oracle is unequivocally focused on a natural cleft or cavern. An oracle of the Gaia at Aegira in Achaia was located in a cave into which the priestess descended to utter prophecy (Pliny *Historia Naturalis* 28.41.147; Pausanias 7.25.13). There was an oracle of Gaia in Olympia, above what is called "the Cave" (Pausanias 5.14.10; Sinn 2000: fig. 2; Parke 1967: 27).

Oracles of Underground Dwellers

The list of seers who uttered gods' orders, not only when alive but also after their death, includes the famous Orpheus and less famous figures such as Trophonius, Amphiaraus, and others. The evidence on the cults of subterranean dwellers reveals a pattern based on a series of common features. Etiological legends on disappearances into chasms and caves vary from place to place, but in most cases vanishing into a chasm is a divine blessing, rendering a mortal hero immortal. These tales look like explanations invented to account for the daimon's life in the depth of the earth: myths that give reasons for an ancient cult type. The status of these characters is that of extreme liminality: they belong neither to the living nor to the dead nor to the gods. Thus, they are able to act as mediators between the worlds, disclosing to the living secret knowledge normally confined to the dead or to the gods (Ustinova 2002, with refs).

Trophonius, whose oracle was in Lebadeia (Boeotia), was also believed to have vanished there beneath the earth. From then on, he lived in a cave under a hill as an oracular god.[2] The oracle in Lebadeia already existed by the sixth century BC. In both literary and epigraphic sources, the act of consultation of the oracle is described as descent—*catabasis*. We are lucky to possess both a detailed description of the procedure there by Pausanias (9.39.1–40.1), and a unique account of the enquirer's experience by Plutarch, in the dialogue *The Daimonion of Socrates* (*Moralia* 590B–592F).

The preparation for the consultation took several days and included not only preliminary sacrifices, but also secluded lodging in a small building, cold baths, prayers, special diet, and sexual abstinence, as well as music and dancing. Only when well-prepared for the tremendous experience—that is, exhausted, tense with anticipation, and disposed to hallucinating—did the consulter

descend to Trophonius' cave. The symbolism of the Trophonium was that of the netherworld: at night two boys personifying Hermes, the conductor of the souls to Hades, led the inquirer to the oracular cave (Bonnechere 2003: 139–64; 236–48). The prophetic grotto was most probably an artificial circular hole, several meters deep: the inquirer lay on the ground, and then, according to Pausanias, he was swiftly drawn into another hole, as if by an eddy (Pausanias 9.39.11). The inner space appears to have been a small recess at the bottom of the larger grotto, where only the feet of the consulter entered, while he remained stretched out on the floor (Bonnechere 2003: 159–63). In fact, the image of the whirl could derive from the vortex experienced by the inquirers at the beginning of their prophetic trance—that is, altered state of consciousness—induced by the immersion into the dark coolness of the grotto.

Plutarch's description of the consulter's experience in the Trophonium is a fascinating account of the communication of a young man named Timarchus, who spent two nights and a day in the cave, in a world beyond normal experience. He could not discern whether he was awake or dreaming, but it seemed to him that after passing through profound darkness, he was struck on the head, "the sutures parted and released his soul." In a sleep or in trance, Timarchus' soul flew above an ocean with shining isles, and in a mixture of joyfulness and awe he heard voices that explained to him the mystery of metempsychosis and predicted his imminent death (Hani 1975; Babut 1984; Bonnechere 2003: 154–64).

The most substantial inference from Plutarch's description is that an inquirer in the Trophonium lived through an out-of-body experience: lack of awareness of the surroundings, passage through darkness to translucent and pure light, flight over a magnificent country, visual and auditory hallucinations, feeling of unearthly happiness, and the final gift of clairvoyance. Quite predictably, Timarchus' altered state of consciousness was accompanied by culturally patterned visions, reflecting Greek religious and philosophical ideas, such as mythical geography of the netherworld, as well as the notions of the soul, its liberty, and need of purification. The variance in the kind of hallucinations experienced in the Trophonium was known to Pausanias (9.39.11), who observes that inside the cavern different inquirers learn the future in different ways, sometimes by sight and at other times by hearing. Thus, the oracle of Trophonius presents an example of direct inspiration of the inquirers by a deity, which took place in the closed space of the grotto, after complex preparation.

Regrettably, this detailed account is the exception to the rule: testimony on other oracular centers consists of indirect allusions or brief hints to altered states of consciousness experienced by consulters or personnel. However, the evidence on the Trophonium suggests that under similar conditions, namely cultic preparations, isolation inside a cave, and religious awe, ancient Greek consulters would have attained similar experiences and interpreted them in a similar way.

The baffling status of the immortal subterranean daimons who do not fit into any of the usual Greek categories, and the artificial provision of mythical explanations of their cults' focus on prophecy and initiations, suggest that it was the firm connection to the caves and underground chambers that constituted the core of the cult. This core, revelation of hidden knowledge in a cave, could not be changed; it had therefore to be explained and preserved (Ustinova 2002).

The Apolline Prophecy

No other Olympian could be farther from the subterranean world (Plutarch *Moralia* 566C), but it was Apollo who returned there time and again, prophesying from the darkness of natural caves and artificial grottos. The god of arts is even portrayed standing near the *omphalos* inside a vault, presumably the Delphic grotto, on the famous relief by Archelaos of Priene, known as "Apotheosis of Homer" (Richter 1969: fig. 248).

The sanctuary of Apollo at Claros in Asia Minor was associated with prophecy from a very early date (Robert 1967: 306–8; Parke 1985: 219–24). The mantic session at Claros was held in a grotto (Tacitus *Annales* 2.54, Pliny *Historia Naturalis* 2.232). The lifestyle of the medium comprised seclusion, purifications, fasting, and other austerities, and indeed the strain of possession by the god. The underground holy of holies consists of two chambers with a passage between them (Robert 1967: 309–10, fig. 117; Bean 1979: 158–9; Parke 1985: 138). In the almost total darkness, this intricate passage must have given the impression of a maze. Influenced by his faith, the confusing subterranean passage, and by purifications he had undergone before entering the grotto, he drank the sacred water and started singing (Iamblichus *De mysteriis* 3.11). In modern terms, at Claros the medium attained altered state of consciousness due to the effect of his descent into the underground grotto, enhanced by earlier preparations.

In the sanctuary of Apollo Ptoios on Mt Ptoion in Boeotia, behind the temple was an artificial grotto (Guillon 1943: 96; 137, 140, pl. 14.). An early third-century BC hexameter inscription on a base of a statue dedicated to Apollo Ptoios provides valuable information on the mantic procedure at the sanctuary. The god described as "nightly" appeared to the dedicant in the gloomy grotto, and inspired his revelation. The contact between the god and the mortal at Ptoion is pictured as a direct encounter, the communication including not only auditory, but also visual messages (Guillon 1943: 109–10, 144; Guillon 1946). It seems that the prophet attained his visions in an ecstatic state, which affected his articulation, at least on some occasions, as Herodotus' story of the prophecy given to the Persian Mys hints (Herodotus 8.135; Robert 1950; Schachter 1981–94: 1: 66).

At Nea Paphos on Cyprus, Apollo Hylates is mentioned in two fourth-century BC syllabic inscriptions placed at the entrance and within a cave, actually a rock-cut tomb furnished for the god's use by the dedicant of the complex (Mitford 1960; Mlynarczyk 1980). Oracular activities are likely to have been performed at the site. The conversion of an abandoned tomb into Apollo's shrine would be unthinkable if it had not been done in accordance with the demands of the god's cult.

The middle of the Greek world was in Delphi. It was marked with the *omphalos*, the umbilical midpoint of the universe. The heart of Delphi was a cavern, which accommodated the *omphalos* and the seat of the greatest of the Greek oracles. Although only few were allowed into "the innermost part of the temple," the ceremony of oracle-giving has never been a secret from the public: not only Delphic clergy attended it, but also the inquirers themselves, after they had performed the customary purifications and sacrifices (Parke and Wormell 1956: 1, 17). Ancient authors referred to this ceremony freely, and painters depicted it on vases. Prophecy was delivered by a simple woman from Delphi, known as the Pythia. The Pythia had to live in isolation from all contact and relation with strangers, to forestall any emotion which would interfere with her function as a mouthpiece of the god. Having purified herself, the Pythia entered the holy of holies in the innermost part of the temple known as the *adyton* ("space not to be entered"). The adyton contained the *omphalos*, a round stone believed to designate the navel of the world, a laurel tree, a golden statue of Apollo, and a tripod, which the Pythia mounted during the oracular session (Courby 1927: 59–69, fig. 61; Roux 1976: 134–5, figs 7 and 8; Roux 2000: 195, fig. 13; Parke 1939: 22; 27–30; Delcourt 1981: 42; Green 1989: 110).

Inspired by Apollo, the Pythia responded to the questions posed by inquirers (Parke 1939: 32; Parke and Wormell 1956: 1, 34–40; Flacelière 1938: 76–9; Roux 1976: 64–84; Latte 1940; Maurizio 1995; 1998). After the Pythia had been asked the question, she entered an altered state of consciousness, known to the Greeks as prophetic *mania* (Rohde 1925: 312–13; Dodds 1973: 65–101; Maurizio 1995: 70–9; Delcourt 1981: 54–5; Roux 1976: 157). Although possessed by the god, she was neither frenzied nor hysterical. In both painted and verbal depictions, she appears calm and concentrated. Her utterance, heard by the consulters present in the adyton, was articulate and could be rendered in verse or in prose, even if the meaning remained obscure: the oracular Apollo was *Loxias*, "the ambiguous" (Strabo 9.3.5; Amandry 1950: 164; Delcourt 1981: 54–5; Roux 1976: 157; Maurizio 1995: 70).

Since the fifth century BC the written tradition refers to the Delphic adyton, holy of holies, as an artificial vault, located below the floor level of the rest of the temple. Athenian dramatists describe the god living in this grotto: in Aeschylus' trilogy *Oresteia*, the Delphic Apollo is praised as "[the god] who dwells in the great well-built cavern" (Aeschylus *Choephori* 797, cf. 803–5; 954; *Eumenides* 180; Euripides *Ion* 220–9, 233, 245; *Andromache* 1093; *Phoenissae* 237). The Boeotian poet Pindar returns to the same image (*Pythian Odes* 5.68, 8.63). In Aristonoos' hymn, composed in the fourth century BC, the Corinthian poet mentions "the inner recess in the umbilical center of the earth and the Delphic laurel tree" (Furley and Bremer 2001: 1: 116–18; 2: 38–45)

The Delphic cavern is pictured as a man-made vault. If indeed it is so, the fact that the cavity in the Delphic adyton was artificial does not contradict other testimonies and does not indicate that it was not used in the mantic procedure. Actually, in Trophonius' oracle at Lebadeia and in Apollo's sanctuary at Claros, the grottos in which consulters descended were also man-made.

The first accounts of the prophetic breath in the adyton are Hellenistic: "the breath," *pneuma*, emanating from the earth through a chasm in the adyton, is considered to be a material substance inspiring the Pythia to utter oracles (Strabo 9.3.5; Pseudo-Longinus *On the sublime* 13.2; cf. Diodorus of Sicily 16.26). At the beginning of the second century AD, Plutarch witnessed the Pythia's behavior and the layout of the Delphic temple directly during his long service there as a priest. These subjects are mentioned by Plutarch in two dialogues, *The Oracles at Delphi No Longer Given in Verse* and *The Obsolescence of Oracles*. The testimony of Plutarch, who had profound first-hand knowledge of the Delphic ritual, and wrote for people he could hardly deceive on these matters, attests to the same three basic elements of the action in the holy of holies as described by Strabo: a hollow, emanations, and the subsequent mantic inspiration of the Pythia (*Moralia* 397C, 404F, 437C–D; Flacelière 1943; 1947; 1962; Schröder 1990; Jaillard 2007).[3]

Until the beginning of the twentieth century, this tradition had never been questioned. The archaeological excavations in Delphi, which yielded no substantial remains of the adyton (Courby 1927: 65–6; Will 1942/43: 16; Bourguet 1914: 249–50; Roux 1976: 93), brought about a completely different approach to the reconstruction of the prophetic séance (Oppé 1904). The prevailing opinion now was that neither subterranean hollows nor gases affecting the mental state of the Pythia ever existed in the adyton (Will 1942/43; Amandry 1950: 215–30; Fontenrose 1978: 197; Parke 1939: 21; Nilsson 1961–1967: 1, 172; Dietrich 1978: 6; Rosenberger 2001: 53). As a result, the entire ancient tradition had to be explained away, and this task was ingeniously carried out by several scholars (Poulsen 1920: 22–3; Will 1942/43: 174; Flacelière 1965: 51; Roux 1976: 156–7; Dodds 1973: 73; Lloyd-Jones 1976: 67; Parke 1967: 80; Green 1989: 102).

This skepticism is astonishing. In 458 BC, when Aeschylus' trilogy *Oresteia* was staged, some of the people in the audience had attended mantic séances in Delphi: we know about official Athenian delegations to Delphi during the first decades of the fifth century BC, to say nothing about private persons who also consulted the oracle. All these inquirers visited the adyton and were present at the Pythia's prophesying. Even if Aeschylus had wished to invent or lie about the Delphic adyton, he would not have been able to mislead his audience on this subject. In the *Eumenides* the god himself appears twice in his oracular shrine, "the bright god who dwells in the cave" (verse 221). How could Apollo be placed in the wrong surroundings? The idea to attribute a nook in the earth to the "bright god" would be bizarre, unless the audience knew about the subterranean vault. And why would a pious Athenian poet wish to fabricate details concerning the sacred Delphic temple? It seems much more probable and simple to hold that, in the fifth century BC, there was an artificial vault in the Delphic adyton.

Moreover, the first French excavators have already taken note of the fact that only meager traces of the adyton had been preserved, and that these remains did not contradict the traditional image of the temple (Courby 1927: 47–80; Roux 1976: 94). Although there was no trace of a natural cleft below the temple floor, indications of the existence of an artificial grotto were discovered: the area, indicated by the break in the pavement near the back wall of the temple, is sunken, lying more than two meters below the surrounding floor (Courby 1927: 66, fig. 55; Roux 1976: 110; Suárez de la Torre 2005: 22). Recent geological discoveries in the area of Delphi have succeeded in identifying the prophetic vapor and in demonstrating that both fracturing and emissions of intoxicating gases occurred under the temple of Apollo (de Boer and Hale 2001; de Boer et al. 2001; Spiller et al. 2002). These gases, methane and ethane and ethylene, are colorless and can produce mild narcotic effects. Ethylene in particular was used as a surgical anesthetic till the 1970s, and in light doses, it allows full control of the body, but creates a sensation of euphoria (Hale et al. 2003; de Boer et al. 2001).[4]

Thus, after a century of disbelief, the ancient tradition declared "unsatisfactory" has been proven to offer quite an accurate account of the layout of the temple and ritual at Delphi. Yet notwithstanding the reassessment of the ancient tradition on *pneuma*, testimonies regarding the existence of a submerged vault in the Delphic adyton are still misinterpreted, and only a few authors acknowledge the role of *pneuma* in Pythia's inspiration (Mikalson 2005: 106; Ogden 2001: 245; Curnow 2004: 56; Bowden 2005: 19). Thus, it is essential that written accounts of the layout of the Delphic adyton are basically coherent in their own right, and cannot be disregarded in their entirety as fallacious nuisance.

It is clear now that at Delphi the holy of holies was an artificial grotto. There the Pythia experienced a state of trance, which was induced by inhalation of hydrocarbon gases emitted from the fissure in the bedrock. The whole temple appears to have been erected in order to take in a strip of the prophetic ground. The chasm connects the holy of holies to the depth of the earth. The *omphalos* represents the navel of the

Fig I The ruins of the Temple of Apollo at Delphi (Photo: Paul Devereux)

world, while the laurel tree symbolizes its summit, and from this tree Apollo himself speaks. Accordingly, the inner sanctum of the Delphic temple, considered the umbilical center of the cosmos, comprises its two extremities, linking the highest and the lowest spheres. The action in the adytum is focused on the Pythia, who conveys the words of the god. Thus, similarly to many other prophetic caves, the Delphic cavern served as a place where the medium attained altered states of consciousness, but unlike most other oracular centers, the method employed there relied on the use of narcotic gases rather than on sensory deprivation.

Interpretation

We have seen that a great number of Greek oracular cults focused on caves, irrespective of the divergent nature of the divine patrons of these cults. In some instances, the association with caves may be explained, at least superficially, by recourse to the divine personalities of the gods. For instance, the Nymphs were the deities of wild nature, dwelling in caves. What could be more self-evident than to ascribe to their power those cases of trance, sometimes prophetic or poetic, which occurred in caves to people isolated from society and from the light of day? Another category of prophecy given in

Time and Mind   Volume 2—Issue 3—November 2009, pp. 265–286

caves is connected to the chthonic realm. Myth tended to place entrances to the netherworld in multiple caves, and many among them became seats of prominent oracles, where predictions were given either by the dead or by deities of the netherworld. However, the issue becomes more complicated when we move on to oracles belonging to Apollo, whose personality was not connected with the chthonic realm. It would be logically fallacious to devise an individual explanation for each instance of prophecy in caves. It may be assumed that the fundamental reason for locating prophetic activities in caves was the need of the gods' mediums to attain divine inspiration, that is, to alter their state of consciousness.

Ages-long experience had taught the Greeks to induce altered states of consciousness by a variety of means, and for the purposes of divination they used at least two methods. The easiest and universally applicable technique was sensory deprivation. In the geographic setting of Greece, caverns and grottos provided an easy way to achieve total or almost-total isolation.

The second method required special geological conditions, namely, a source of poisonous gas having a euphoriant or psychotropic effect. It is essential that the gas be inhaled in sufficient concentration, therefore in a closed space. Natural combination of these requirements was provided by clefts opening into caves in the Meander valley, whereas in Delphi the prophetic gas was to be inhaled inside an artificial grotto.

Inspired divination was in many cases based on direct contact between the god and the consulter. Even if we assume that at the sanctuary of Trophonius inquirers

who did not appear likely candidates for surrender to trance were segregated at the stage of preliminary ceremonies, their number remained limited. Cases of alteration of consulters' consciousness and ensuing reports of divine revelations must have been common enough to allow institutions like this oracular center to operate smoothly. Apparently visitors to caves sacred to the Nymphs did not necessarily become nympholepts, but their trances were sufficiently frequent to inspire numerous jokes and allusions. Thus, cave experiences of ordinary Greeks were quite widespread.

In addition, well-established oracular centers like Delphi and Claros employed full-time intermediaries of the gods. Although the neurological mechanisms of their trances and revelations did not differ from those of laymen, their ascetic lifestyle, expertise, and natural proclivity allowed them to manipulate their consciousness much more efficiently. As a result, their predictions were especially impressive and well-known—as well as their oracular techniques. Prophetic priests, members of sacred embassies, sent to Delphi and Claros by cities all over the Mediterranean, private consulters who applied to these oracles for advice, and individuals who personally experienced altered states of consciousness in caves—all these people knew that descent into caves evoked noetic sensations.

Thus, caves were instrumental in stimulating altered states of consciousness in two ways, either as places of isolation causing sensory deprivation, or as closed spaces allowing inhalation of narcotic gases in appropriate dosage. This psychotropic or, in the opinion of the Greeks, numinous quality of the caves was common knowledge to such a degree that the association of seers and prophets with caves became universal.

Notes

1 This and related subjects are treated in detail in my book on Greek cave experiences (Ustinova 2009). The research was supported by the Israel Science Foundation (Grant No. 557/05).

2 The most systematic and profound research on Trophonius was conducted by P. Bonnechere (2003). For the oracle and its history, see also Schachter 1967; Schachter 1981–94: 3, 66–89; Schachter 1984; Clark 1968.

3 The reliability of Roman authors on Delphic matters has been even more sweepingly refuted by scholars, than that of the Greek writers. Re-reading of the pertinent passages in Latin literature (e.g. Lucan Pharsalia 5. 67–236, cf. Bayet 1946: 69; Cicero De divinatione 1. 19. 38; 1. 36. 79; 1. 50. 115) demonstrates however that this approach is based on a preconception.

4 A different approach to the location of the faults and the nature of gaseous emissions is suggested by Etiope et al. (2006). These studies have recently been questioned by D. Lehoux (2007), whose criticism is based mainly on a return to the century-long refusal to accept ancient evidence of the existence of a chasm and gases in Delphi at its face value. Moreover, Lehoux's arguments are compromised by his prima facie antagonism regarding the line of interpretation used by J. Z. de Boer, G. Etiope and their teams. In Lehoux', opinion, any attempt to account for ancient religious phenomena using results of modern science is methodologically erroneous. This approach, based on the understanding of human beings as social actors separated from their biological nature, limits historical research. Although at present the exact composition of the "oracular breath" at Delphi may not be established exactly, it is essential that geological and physiological aspects of oracle-giving in Delphi be studied along with written and archaeological evidence.

References

Amandry, P., 1950. *La Mantique apollinienne à Delphes*. Paris: Boccard.

Amandry, P., 1984. "Le culte des nymphes et de Pan à l'antre Corycien." *Bulletin de correspondance hellénique* Suppl. 9: 395–425.

Andresen, J., 2001. "Conclusion: Religion in the Flesh: Forging New Methodologies for the Study of Religion." in J. Andresen (ed.), *Religion in Mind: Cognitive Perspectives on Religious Belief, Ritual, and Experience*. Cambridge: Cambridge University Press, 257–87.

Austin, J., 1998. *Zen and the Brain: Toward and Understanding of Meditation and Consciousness*. Cambridge, MA and London: MIT Press.

Babut, D., 1984. "Le dialogue de Plutarque 'Sur le démon de Socrate.' Essai d'interprétation." *Bulletin d'Association Guillaume Budé:* 51–76.

Bayet, J., 1946. "La Mort de la Pythie: Lucain, Plutarque et la chronologie delphique." *Mélanges dédiés à la mémoire de Félix Crat*. Paris. 1: 53–76.

Bean, G. E., 1979. *Aegean Turkey*. London: J. Murray.

Bean, G. E., 1989. *Turkey Beyound the Meander*. London: E. Benn.

Blacker, C., 1975. "Other World Journeys in Japan." in H.R.E. Davidson (ed.), *The Journey to the Other World*. Cambridge: Brewer/Rowman/Littlefield, pp. 42–72.

Blackmore, S., 1993. *Dying to Live: Near-Death Experiences*. Buffalo, NY: Prometheus.

Bonnechere, P., 2003. *Trophonios de Lébadée*. Leiden: Brill.

Borgeaud, P., 1988. *The Cult of Pan in Ancient Greece*. Chicago and London: University of Chicago Press.

Bouché-Leclercq, A., 1879–82. *Histoire de la divination*. Paris: Leroux.

Bourguet, E., 1914. *Les ruines de Delphes*. Paris: Fontemoing.

Bowden, H., 2005. *Classical Athens and the Delphic Oracle*. Cambridge: Cambridge University Press.

Brommer, F., 1956. "Pan." *Pauly-Wissowa Realencyclopädie für Altertumswissenschaft Suppl.* 8: 949–1008.

Burkert, W., 2005. "Mantik in Griechenland." *Thesaurus Cultus et Rituum Antiquorum.* Los Angeles: Getty Publications, 3: 1–51.

Chadwick, N.K., 1942. *Poetry and Prophecy.* Cambridge: Cambridge University Press.

Clark, R.J., 1968. "Trophonios: The Manner of His Revelation." *Transactions of the American Philological Association* 99: 63–75.

Clottes, J., 2004. "Hallucinations in Caves." *Cambridge Archaeological Journal* 14(1): 81–2.

Connor, W.R., 1988. "Seized by the Nymphs: Nympholepsy and Symbolic Expression in Classical Greece." *Classical Antiquity* 7(2): 155–89.

Cornford, F.M., 1952. *Principium Sapientiae: The Origins of Greek Philosophical Thought.* Cambridge: Cambridge University Press.

Courby, F., 1927. *Fouilles de Delphes. Vol. II. La terrasse du temple.* Paris.

Cross, T.M. and Aaronson, S., 1988. "The Vapours of One Entrance to Hades." *Antiquity* 62: 88–9.

Curnow, T., 2004. *The Oracles of the Ancient World.* London: Duckworth.

D'Aquili, E. and Newberg, A.B., 1998. "The Neuropsychological Basis of Religions, Or Why God Won't Go Away." *Zygon* 33(2): 187–201.

de Bernardi Ferraro, D., 1993. "Hierapolis." *Arslantepe, Hierapolis, Iasos, Kyme.* Venice: Marsilio, pp. 105–89.

de Boer, J.Z. and Hale, J.R., 2001. "The Geological Origins of the Oracle at Delphi, Greece." in W.G. McGuire, D.R. Griffiths, P.L. Hancock, and O.S. Stewart (eds), *The Archaeology of Geological Catastrophes.* London: pp. 399–412.

de Boer, J.Z., Hale, J.R., and Chanton, J., 2001. "New Evidence for the Geological Origins of the Ancient Delphic Oracle (Greece)." *Geology* 29(8): 707–10.

Delatte, A., 1934. *Les Conceptions de l'enthousiasme chez les philosophes présocratiques.* Paris: Les Belles Lettres.

Delcourt, M., 1981. *L'Oracle de Delphes.* Paris: Payot.

Devereux, P., 2000. *The Sacred Place: The Ancient Origins of Holy and Mystical Sites.* London: Cassell.

Dietrich, B.C., 1978. "Reflections on the Origins of the Oracular Apollo." *Bulletin of the Institute of Classical Studies* 25: 1–18.

Dodds, E.R., 1973. *The Greeks and the Irrational.* Berkeley, CA: University of California Press.

Edwards, C.M., 1985. *Votive Reliefs to Pan and the Nymphs.* Ph.D. thesis, New York University.

Ellwood, R.S., 1980. *Mysticism and Religion.* Englewood Cliffs, NJ: Prentice Hall.

Etiope, G., Papatheodorou, G., Christodoulou, D., Geraga, M., and Favali, P., 2006. "The Geological Links of the Ancient Delphic Oracle (Greece): A Reappraisal of Natural Gas Occurrence and Origin." *Geology* 10(34): 821–4.

Farnell, L.R., 1907. *The Cults of the Greek States.* Oxford: Clarendon.

Faure, P., 1964. *Fonctions des cavernes crétoises.* Paris: Ecole Française d'Athènes.

Flacelière, R., 1938. "Le fonctionnement de l'oracle de Delphes au temps de Plutarque." *Annales de l'École des Hautes Études de Gand* 2: 69–107.

Flacelière, R., 1943. "Plutarque et la Pythie." *Revue des études grecques* 56: 72–109.

Flacelière, R., 1947. *Plutarque: Sur la disparition des oracles.* Paris: Les Belles Lettres.

Flacelière, R., 1962. *Plutarque: Dialogue sur les oracles de la Pythie. Edition, introduction et commentaire.* Paris: Les Belles Lettres.

Flacelière, R. (1965). *Greek Oracles.* London: Elek Books.

Fontenrose, J., 1978. *The Delphic Oracle.* Berkeley, CA: University of California Press.

Freedman, S.J., Grunebaum, H.U. and Greenblatt, M., 1965. "Perceptual and Cognitive Changes in Sensory Deprivation." in P. Solomon (ed.), *Sensory Deprivation.* Cambridge, MA: Harvard University Press, pp. 58–71.

Furley, W.D. and Bremer, J.M., 2001. *Greek Hymns.* Tübingen: Mohr Siebeck.

Gabbard, G.O. and Twemlow, S.W., 1984. *With the Eyes of the Mind: An Empirical Analysis of Out-of-Body States.* New York: Praeger.

Geels, A., 1982. "Mystical Experience and the Emergence of Creativity." in N.G. Holm (ed.), *Religious Ecstasy.* Stockholm: Almqvist & Wiksell, pp. 27–62.

Gimello, R.M., 1978. "Mysticism and Meditation." in S. Katz (ed.), *Mysticism and Philosophical Analysis.* New York: Sheldon, pp. 170–99.

Gomme, A.W. and Sandbach, F.H., 1973. *Menander. A Commentary.* Oxford: Oxford University Press.

Green, C., 1968. *Out-of-the-Body Experiences.* London: Hamish Hamilton.

Green, P., 1989. *Classical Bearings: Interpreting Ancient History and Culture.* London: Thames & Hudson.

Guillon, P., 1943. *Les Trépieds du Ptoion. 2: Depositif matériel. Signification historique et religieuse.* Paris: Ecole Française d'Athènes.

Guillon, P. 1946. "L'Offrande d'Aristichos et la consultation de l'oracle du Ptoion au début du IIIe s. av. J.-C." *Bulletin de correspondance hellénique* 70: 216–32.

Hale, J.R., de Boer, J.Z., Chanton, J.P. and Spiller, H.A., 2003. "Questioning the Delphic Oracle." *Scientific American,* August.

Hani, J., 1975. "Le Mythe de Timarque chez Plutarque et la structure de l'exstase." *Revue des études grecques* 88: 105–20.

Harner, M., 1990. *The Way of the Shaman.* San Francisco: Harper.

Hastin Bennet, A.M., 1965. "Sensory Deprivation in Aviation." in P. Solomon (ed.), *Sensory Deprivation.* Cambridge MA: Harvard University Press, pp. 161–73.

Herter, H., 1937. "Nymphen." *Pauly-Wissowa Realencyclopädie für Altertumswissenschaft* 17: 1527–81.

Hollenback, J.B., 1996. *Mysticism: Experience, Response, and Empowerment.* University Park, PA: Penn State University Press.

Hood, R.W., Jr., 1997. "The Empirical Study of Mysticism." in B. Spilka and D.N. McIntosh (eds), *The Psychology of Religion.* Boulder, CO and Oxford: Westview, pp. 222–32.

Iversen, L., 2001. *Drugs: A Very Short Introduction.* Oxford: Oxford University Press.

Jaillard, D., 2007. "Plutarque et la divination: la piété d'un prêtre philosophe." *Revue de l'histoire des religions* 24: 149–69.

James, W., 1961. *The Varieties of Religious Experience.* London: Collins.

Joseph, R. (ed.), 2003. *NeuroTheology: Brain, Science, Spirituality, Religious Experience.* San Jose, CA: California University Press.

Jost, M., 1985. *Sanctuaires et cultes d'Arcadie.* Paris: J. Vrin.

Kubie, L.S., 1965. "Theoretical Aspects of Sensory Deprivation." in P. Solomon (ed.), *Sensory Deprivation.* Cambridge, MA: Harvard University Press, pp. 208–20.

La Barre, W., 1980. *Culture in Context.* Durham, NC: Duke University Press.

Larson, J. (1995). "The Corycian Nymphs and Bee Maidens of the Homeric Hymn to Hermes." *Greek, Roman and Byzantine Studies* 36(4): 341–57.

Larson, J., 2001. *Greek Nymphs.* Oxford: Oxford University Press.

Laski, M., 1990. *Ecstasy in Secular and Religious Experiences.* Los Angeles, CA: Jeremy P. Tarcher.

Latte, K., 1940. "The Coming of the Pythia." *Harvard Theological Revue* 33: 9–18.

Lavagne, H., 1988. *Operosa antra: Recherches sur la grotte à Rome de Sylla à Hadrien.* Rome: Ecole française de Rome.

Lehoux, D., 2007. "Drugs and the Delphic Oracle." *Classical World* 101(1): 41–56.

Lewis, I.M., 1989. *Ecstatic Religion: A Study of Shamanism and Spirit Possession*. London and New York: Routledge.

Lewis-Williams, D., 2002. *The Mind in the Cave*. London: Thames & Hudson.

Lex, B.W., 1979. "The Neurobiology of Ritual Trance." in E. D'Aquili, C.D. Laughlin, and J. McManus (eds), *The Spectrum of Ritual*. New York: Columbia University Press, pp. 117–51.

Lilly, J.C., 1972. *The Centre of the Cyclone: An Autobiography of Inner Space*. New York: Julian Press.

Lloyd-Jones, H., 1976. "The Delphic Oracle." *Greece and Rome* 23: 60–73.

Ludwig, A.M., 1968. "Altered States of Consciousness." in R. Prince (ed.), *Trance and Possession States*. Montreal: R.M. Rucke Society, pp. 69–95.

Martindale, C., 1981. *Cognition and Consciousness*. Homewood, IL: Dorsey Press.

Masson, O., 1966. "Kypriaka." *Bulletin de correspondance hellénique* 90: 1–31.

Masson, O., 1981. "A propos des inscriptions chypriotes de Kafizin." *Bulletin de correspondance hellénique* 105: 623–49.

Maurizio, L., 1995. "Anthropology and Spirit Possession: A Reconstruction of the Pythia's Role at Delphi." *Journal of Hellenic Studies* 115: 69–86.

Maurizio, L., 1998. "Narrative, Biographical and Ritual Conventions at Delphi." in I. Chirassi Colombo and T. Seppilli (eds), *Sibille e linguaggi oracolari*. Pisa and Rome: Istituti Editoriali e Poligrafici Internazionali, pp. 133–58.

McGinn, B., 2005. "Visions and Visualizations in the Here and Hereafter." *Harvard Theological Revue* 98(3): 227–46.

Merkur, D., 1985. *Becoming Half Hidden: Shamanism and Initiation Among the Inuit*. Stockholm: Almqvist & Wiksell.

Merkur, D., 1989. "The Visionary Practices of Jewish Apocalyptists." *The Psychoanalytic Study of Society* 14: 119–48.

Merkur, D., 1993. *Gnosis: An Esoteric Tradition of Mystical Visions and Unions*. Albany, NY: State University of New York Press.

Mikalson, J.D., 2005. *Ancient Greek Religion*. Oxford: Blackwell.

Mitford, T.B., 1960. "Paphian Inscriptions Hoffmann Nos. 98 and 99." *Bulletin of the Institute of Classical Studies* 7: 1–10.

Mitford, T.B., 1980. *The Nymphaeum of Kafizin: The Inscribed Pottery*. Berlin and New York: W. de Gruyter.

Mlynarczyk, J., 1980. "The Paphian Sanctuary of Apollo Hylates." *Report of the Department of Antiquities of Cyprus*: 239–52.

Motte, A., 2004. "Le Sacré dans la nature et dans l'homme: la perception du devin chez les Grecs." in J. Ries, A. Motte, and N. Spineto (eds), *Les Civilisations méditerranéens et le sacré*. Turnhout: Brepols, pp. 229–54.

Murray, P., 1981. "Poetic Inspiration in Early Greece." *Journal of Hellenic Studies* 101: 87–100.

Negri, S. and Leucci, G., 2006. "Geophysical Investigation of the Temple of Apollo (Hierapolis, Turkey)." *Journal of Archaeological Science* 33: 1505–13.

Newberg, A.B. and D'Aquili, E., 2000. "The Creative Brain/The Creative Mind." *Zygon* 35(1): 53–68.

Newberg, A., D'Aquili, E. and Rause, V., 2001. *Why God Won't Go Away? Brain Science and the Biology of Belief*. New York: Ballentine.

Nilsson, M.P., 1961–1967. *Geschichte der griecheischen Religion*. Munich: C.H. Beck.

Ogden, D., 2001. *Greek and Roman Necromancy*. Princeton and Oxford: Princeton University Press.

Oppé, A.P., 1904. "The Chasm at Delphi." *Journal of Hellenic Studies* 24: 214–40.

Parke, H.W., 1939. *A History of the Delphic Oracle*. Oxford: Blackwell.

Parke, H.W., 1967. *Greek Oracles*. London: Hutchinson.

Parke, H.W., 1985. *The Oracles of Apollo in Asia Minor*. London: Croom Helm.

Parke, H.W. and Wormell, D.E.W., 1956. *The Delphic Oracle*. Oxford: Blackwell.

Pearson, J.L., 2002. *Shamanism and the Ancient Mind: A Cognitive Approach to Archaeology*. Walnut Creek, CA: AltaMira Press.

Poulsen, F., 1920. *Delphi*. London: Gyldenal.

Ramachandran, V.S. and Blakeslee, S., 1998. *Phantoms in the Brain*. London: Fourth Estate.

Richter, G.M.A., 1969. *A Handbook of Greek Art*. London and New York: Phaidon.

Robert, L., 1950. "Le Carien Mys et l'oracle du Ptöon." *Hellenica VIII*. Paris: A. Maisonneuve, 23–38.

Robert, L., 1967. "L'Oracle de Claros," in C. Delvoye and G. Roux (eds), *La Civilisation grecque*. Bruxelles: Renaissance du livre, pp. 305–12.

Rohde, E., 1925. *Psyche*. London: Kegan, Trench, Trubner.

Rosenberger, V., 2001. *Griechische Orakel: Eine Kulturgeschichte*. Darmstadt: Theiss.

Rosenfeld, B., 1999. "R. Simeon b. Yohai, Wonder Worker and Magician: Scholar, Saddiq and Hasid." *Revue des études juives* 58: 349–84.

Rouget, G., 1990. *La Musique et la trance*. Paris: Gallimard.

Roux, G., 1976. *Delphes: son oracle et ses dieux*. Paris: Les Belles Lettres.

Roux, G., 2000. "L'Architecture à Delphes: un siècle de découvertes." in A. Jacquemin (ed.), *Delphes: Cent ans après la Grande fouille. Essai de bilan*. Paris: Ecole Française d'Athènes, pp. 181–99.

Roux, J.-P., 1999. *Montagnes sacrées, montagnes mythiques*. Paris: Fayard.

Schachter, A., 1967. "A Boeotian Cult Type." *Bulletin of the Institute of Classical Studies* 14: 1–16.

Schachter, A., 1981–94. *Cults of Boeotia*. London: University of London, Institute of Classical Studies.

Schachter, A., 1984. "A Consultation of Trophonios (*IG* 7. 4136)." *American Journal of Philology* 105: 258–70.

Schörner, G. and Goette, H.R., 2004. *Die Pan-Grotte von Vari*. Mainz: Philipp Von Zabern.

Schröder, S., 1990. *Plutarchs Schrift De Pythiae oraculis: Text, Einleitung und Kommentar*. Stuttgart: B.G. Teubner.

Shanon, B., 2002. *The Antipodes of the Mind: Charting the Phenomenology of the Ayahuasca Experience*. Oxford: Oxford University Press.

Shurley, J.T., 1962. "Hallucination in Sensory Deprivation and Sleep Deprivation," in J.L. West (ed.), *Hallucinations*. New York and London: Grune & Stratton, pp. 87–91.

Siikala, A.-L., 1982. "The Siberian Shaman's Technique of Ecstasy." in N.G. Holm (ed.), *Religious Ecstasy*. Stockholm: Almqvist & Wiksell, pp. 103–21.

Sinn, U., 2000. *Olympia*. Princeton: M. Wiener.

Snell, B., 1960. *The Discovery of the Mind: The Greek Origins of European Thought*. New York: Harper Torchbooks.

Solomon, P. (ed.), 1965. *Sensory Deprivation*. Cambridge, MA: Harvard University Press.

Spiller, H.A., Hale, J.R., and de Boer, J.Z., 2002. "The Delphic Oracle: A Multidisciplinary Defense of the Gaseous Vent Theory." *Clinical Toxicology* 40(2): 189–96.

Stace, W.T., 1960. *The Teachings of the Mystics*. New York: New American Library.

Starr, C.G., 1968. "Ideas of Truth in Early Greece." *La Parola del passato* 23: 348–59.

Streng, F.J., 1978. "Language and Mystical Awareness," in S. Katz (ed.), *Mysticism and Philosophical Analysis*. London: Sheldon Press, pp. 141–69.

Suárez de la Torre, E., 2005. "Delphes." *Thesaurus Cultus et Rituum Antiquorum*. Los Angeles: Getty Publications, 3: 16–31.

Suedfeld, P., 1969. "Introduction and Historical Background." in J.P. Zubek (ed.), *Sensory Deprivation: Fifteen Years of Research*. New York: Appleton Century Crofts, pp. 3–15.

Ustinova, Y., 1992–98. "Corybantism: The Nature and Role of an Ecstatic Cult in the Greek Polis." *Horos* 10–12: 503–20.

Ustinova, Y., 2002. "'Either a Daimon, or a Hero, or Perhaps a God:' Mythical Residents of Subterranean Chambers." *Kernos* 15: 267–88.

Ustinova, Y., 2009. *Caves and the Ancient Greek Mind: Descending Underground in the Search for Ultimate Truth.* Oxford: Oxford University Press.

Vernant, J.-P. (ed.), 1974. *Divination et rationalité.* Paris: Editions du Seuil.

Vernon, J.A., McGill, T.E., Gulick, W.L., and Candland, D.K., 1965. "The Effect of Human Isolation upon Some Perceptual and Motor Skills." in P. Solomon (ed.), *Sensory Deprivation.* Cambridge, MA: Harvard University Press, pp. 41–57.

West, L.J., 1975. "A Clinical and Theoretical Overview of Hallucinatory Phenomena." in R.K. Siegel and L.J. West (eds), *Hallucinations: Behavior, Experience, and Theory.* New York: Wiley, pp. 287–311.

Whitehouse, R.D., 2001. "A Tale of Two Caves: The Archaeology of Religious Experience in Mediterranean Europe." in P.F. Biehl and F. Bertemes (eds), *The Archaeology of Cult and Religion.* Budapest: Archaeolingua Foundation, pp. 161–7.

Wickens, J.M., 1986. *The Archaeology and History of Cave Use in Attica, Greece, from Late Prehistoric*

Through Roman Times, Ph.D. thesis, Indiana University.

Will, E., 1942/43. "Sur la nature du pneuma delphique." *Bulletin de correspondance hellénique* 66/67: 161–75.

Winkelman, M., 2000. *Shamanism: The Neural Ecology of Consciousness and Healing.* Westport, CT: Bergin & Garvey.

Winkelman, M., 2002. "Shamanism as Neurotheology and Evolutionary Psychology." *American Behavioral Scientist* 45(12): 1873–85.

Winkelman, M., 2004. "Shamanism as the Original Neurotheology." *Zygon* 39(1): 193–217.

Wulff, D.M., 1997. *Psychology of Religion.* New York: Wiley.

Zintzen, C., 1967. *Damascii Vitae Isidori Reliquiae.* Heidelsheim: G. Olms.

Zubek, J.P. (ed.), 1969. *Sensory Deprivation: Fifteen Years of Research.* New York: Appleton Century Crofts.

Zuckerman, M., 1969. "Hallucinations, Reported Sensations, and Images." in J.P. Zubek (ed.), *Sensory Deprivation: Fifteen Years of Research.* New York: Appleton Century Crofts, pp. 85–125.

Time and Mind: The Journal of Archaeology, Consciousness and Culture

Volume 2—Issue 3
November 2009
pp. 287–312
DOI: 10.2752/175169609X12464529903173

Reprints available directly from the publishers

Photocopying permitted by license only

From Boulder to Mountain and Back Again: Self-similarity between Landscape and Mindscape in Cherokee Thought, Speech, and Action as Expressed by the Judaculla Rock Petroglyphs

Johannes Loubser

Johannes Loubser is an archaeologist/rock-art specialist at Stratum Unlimited LLC in Alpharetta, Georgia, USA. His main research interest is integrating ethnography and archaeology, preferably in terms of core beliefs held by direct descendants of those who formed the archaeological record. Among his published work is *Archaeology: the Comic* (2003) and *Mountains, Pools, and Dry Ones among Venda-speaking Chiefdoms of Southern Africa* (2008). jloubser@stratumunlimited.com

Abstract

Located in the Balsam Mountains of west-central North Carolina in the southeastern United States, a prominent petroglyph boulder known as Judaculla Rock has featured prominently in the religious experiences, beliefs, and rituals of the Cherokee people since history was recorded for this part of the world in the nineteenth century. Archaeologically, stratigraphically, and ethnohistorically, the pecked designs and cupules postdate and probably have very little to do with the Late Archaic soapstone quarrying of the boulder. By looking at Judaculla

Rock in the context of the surrounding late prehistoric and protohistoric archaeological sites, landscape, and ethnographic setting, it is possible to develop new understandings concerning the late prehistory and early history of this portion of the Balsam Mountains.

Keywords: petroglyphs, Cherokees, southeastern Indians, altered states of consciousness, spirit helpers, picture maps

Introduction

The primary proposition of this article is that a petroglyph site, like most other archaeological sites, is better understood in its broader religious and landscape contexts. Any evaluation of a religious context should include the experiences (thoughts and emotions that are encountered and formulated internally), beliefs (thoughts shared and transmitted via speech with others), and rituals (shared experiences and beliefs expressed in a culturally sanctioned series of actions) of the people who made the petroglyphs. The ancestors of the Iroquoian-speaking Cherokee Indians of the Blue Ridge Mountains are the most likely candidates for making the petroglyphs on Judaculla Rock (Loubser and Frink 2008), which is the example used in this article (see Fig 1 for the site's location within the southeastern United States). As will be shown in this article, the petroglyph boulder is uniquely placed at a transition point on the landscape, between populated floodplains to the north and west and sparsely populated valleys to the south and east.

A secondary proposition of this article is that similar sets of Cherokee beliefs are expressed at different scales on the

landscape. From macrocosm to microcosm these scales are: the surrounding terrain (associated natural and cultural features, including trails, drainages, camps, and villages); the surrounding site (site morphology and nearby resources, such as significant plants and animals); the rock support (rock morphology, integration between motifs and rock surface, overlap of motifs, reuse of sites, and motif differences). The interplay between these scales of reference in the natural and cultural worlds probably reenforced the very same experiences, beliefs, and actions of the Cherokee Indians that reflected and help modify the landscape in the first instance. All in all, this article shows that without close observation of the associated natural and cultural setting, much of the physical evidence in the landscape and on the boulder would remain meaningless or even go unnoticed.

Fig 1 Map of the southeastern United States showing the location of Judaculla Rock

Landscape Setting

Judaculla Rock is located approximately four miles south of US 107, in Jackson County, North Carolina (Fig 2).

The 20-square-meter sized boulder (Fig 3) is a bedrock outcrop of intrusive meta-ultramafic soapstone (Brown 1985, Pratt and Lewis 1905) in a location where two types of softer gneiss meet. This is in an area where the toe slope of Coward Mountain cuts into the Caney Fork Creek Valley to create a gateway beyond which the valley narrows considerably; the boulder with its petroglyphs is like an engraved post on the eastern side of a natural gate.

Like many other petroglyph locales in the southeastern United States (see e.g. Loubser 2005: 149, Wagner 1996: 75), Judaculla Rock occurs next to an old Indian trail (Tom Hatley, personal communication; see e.g. Parris 1950b: 37; Wilburn 1952b: 21). This trail connected Cherokee settlements in the Caney Fork Creek and Tuckasegee

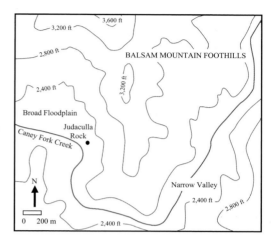

Fig 2 Judaculla Rock as Indicated on the USGS Tuckasegee Topo Map

River valleys with the uplands around Richland Balsam, Haywood Gap, and Tanasee Bald ("bald" being a term given to treeless mountaintops). The southwest to northeast trending Judaculla Ridge, sandwiched by

Fig 3 Photograph of Judaculla Rock showing immediately surrounding terrain (photo: Scott Ashcraft)

the headwaters of the Caney Fork Creek some 10 kilometers southeast of Judaculla Rock, was the landform which connected the populated valleys to the northwest with the comparatively isolated ridge crests and mountaintop balds to the southeast. The diverse ecological setting of Judaculla Rock attracted Native American Indians for millennia, as attested by the surrounding soapstone quarry site and a prehistoric and early historic period Indian site on the Caney Fork Creek floodplain to the northwest. Euro-Americans had chosen to settle in the area by the early nineteenth century. Patches of anomalous vegetation in the area bear testimony of both Native American Indian and Euro-American disturbance of the landscape.

Stands of red cedar trees (*Juniperus virginiana*), also known as cedar, are found scattered in the mountains to the east of Judaculla Rock (Bret Riggs, personal communication). These mountains are known as the Balsams. Of note is a definite line of cedars immediately below a line of cliffs directly east and upslope from Judaculla Rock. According to Tom Hatley (personal communication) red cedar occurs not only below such cliff faces but also in weathered soils, in and around prehistoric sites, and in historic eighteenth- and nineteenth-century farmsteads and yards.

Mooney (1992: 421) states that with "the Cherokee, as with nearly all other tribes east and west, the cedar is held sacred above all other trees. The reasons for this reverence are easily found in its ever-living green, its balsamic fragrance, and the beautiful color of its fine-grained wood." Cherokees add green twigs to a fire in the belief that the sweet fragrance will expel malignant spirits from dreams. One story recalls that the red color of the wood came from the severed head of an anti-social sorcerer who was captured and killed in a cave. Indians tied the decapitated head to the top of a cedar tree and eventually the trickling blood permanently stained the trunk below.

The red wood of cedar trees exudates fragrant oil. Burning cedar logs create a big, hot, intense, and bright-red fire, much different than burning hardwoods or other conifers like pine. The distinctive odor, color, and burn qualities, plus the resin of a red cedar itself, were most probably significant and used in prehistoric times. Moreover, there are cases of anthropogenically maintained cedar groves, today occurring in residual clumps (i.e., descendant trees, minus the original planters and users) (Lee Newsom, personal communication). The occurrence of red cedars in the vicinity of Judaculla Rock is accordingly an indication of a culturally transformed landscape.

The presence of river canebrakes near Judaculla Rock is also culturally significant. Caney Fork Creek apparently got its name from the river cane that grows in the valley (Jerry Parker, personal communication). River cane (*Arundinaria gigantea*) is native to the United States of America and was once abundant in the southeastern states, growing on the floodplains of low-energy rivers and streams. Within this overall setting, the preference of river cane is for micro-landforms that are higher, such as soil ridges. Black Walnut (*Juglans nigra*), Sycamore (*Planatus occidentalis*), and Jewelweed (*Impatiens capensis*) are known to grow within canebrakes. River cane can grow up to a height of 6 meters with a diameter of 2.54 cm. Cherokees and their southeastern Indian neighbors used river canebrakes for a variety of purposes, such as convenient locales for hunting, sources of raw material for basket and mat manufacture, and sites for rituals.

Indians liked to hunt in canebrakes considering that these places were frequented by bears, deer, panthers, wildcats, turkeys, and other small game. Indian artisans would furthermore overnight at canebrakes so that they could harvest and process the river cane to make their baskets and mats. They stayed at these canebrake camps for the duration of the cutting, splitting, peeling, stripping, trimming, and drying of the strips that they called straws. The Cherokee divided the canes into long, thin, narrow splinters, which they dyed (Adair 1930: 456). The mid-nineteenth-century trader Adair (ibid.) described the inside and outside of a Cherokee basket as "covered with a beautiful variety of pleasing figures." According to him these baskets were highly valued, including by European colonists living across the mountains in South Carolina. The Cherokees and their Muskogee-speaking Creek Indian neighbors also wove carpets and mats from split canes.

The mid- to late nineteenth-century naturalist Bartram (1955: 358) noted that the Creeks arranged the split canes of their sacred fire in an oblique cross-like fashion. Bartram also saw flutes made from cane and cedarwood. These flutes were used to make music during certain ceremonies, along with drums and rattles. During the annual first fruit ritual, generally known as the Green Corn Dance among Cherokees, or Busk among the Creeks, the presiding person is still referred to as "Master of Breath," considering that he blows through a section of river cane to empower the medicines

(Swanton 2000: 482). The southeastern Indians also believe that their apical deity blew souls into people when they were created. In this regard the Creek say that "when he blows, the god that is in him goes into the medicine from the soul of the blower" (Swanton 2000: 608).

By 1812 the Coward family had settled on Caney Fork Creek (Parris 1950a). The Cowards were among the first Euro-American pioneers to settle in the mountains of North Carolina and who learned the language of the Iroquoian-speaking Cherokee Indians who had lived in the valley for many generations. One outcome of living so close to Cherokees was that the settlers became acquainted with much of the indigenous traditions and customs (Parris 1950a).

Elderly descendants of Euro-American settlers in the neighborhood where Judaculla Rock is located told Wilburn (1950a: 21) that according to their grandparents "large groups of Cherokee Indians used to assemble at the rock, and remain for a day or two. Solemn ceremonies or rituals would be carried on. The older members of the group with a long cane as a pointer would indicate different objects on the rock, and this would be followed by exclamations and animated chants. These visitations were likely as late as the 1880s and 1890s. The leaders of the groups, as well as some of the others, came from the West [Oklahoma] long after the Removal of 1838." An interesting activity mentioned in this account is the use of the nearby river cane to point at the petroglyphs on the boulder. This action suggests that the boulder and river cane are related; as will be shown below, like the river cane, the boulder also has religious connotations. Cherokees apparently still visit Judaculla Rock in small

Fig 4 Reduced re-drawing of the Judaculla Rock tracing

groups or individually, often in secret, and occasionally leaving behind gifts to the spirits.

Archaeological evidence suggests that prior to having being pecked and engraved the boulder was used for soapstone-bowl extraction. It is to soapstone quarry activities that the discussion now turns, primarily to show that these activities predate the production of petroglyphs at Judaculla Rock and similar boulders in the American southeast.

Archaeological Setting

Soapstone's soft yet durable nature makes it easy to carve and efficient to use. This rock type is particularly well-suited for cooking, as it holds and radiates heat without breaking. In the prehistoric archaeological record of the southeastern United States, soapstone has had a long history as cooking stones and banner stones prior to the manufacture of soapstone bowls. The stratigraphic occurrence of soapstone bowls recovered from deposits above early pottery bowls, in addition to direct radiocarbon dates of soot on soapstone bowls from sites in the coastal plain and piedmont of South Carolina and Georgia, show that soapstone cooking bowls postdate their ceramic equivalents by roughly four centuries (Elliott 1986; Sassaman 1997).

Whereas soapstone bowls date to around 3,600 years ago, the earliest ceramics are 4,000 years old. In the mountainous areas of Georgia and North Carolina, however, soapstone-bowl manufacture predates ceramics, baked-clay vessels appearing in the archaeological record only 3,000 years ago. Based on excavated stratigraphic associations with Early Woodland ceramics, archaeologists such as Dickens and Carnes (1983) have proposed that soapstone quarries in the piedmont and mountains continued to be worked into the Early Woodland, but not later. Prehistoric evidence for the cessation of soapstone-bowl production, together with the absence of primary soapstone-bowl manufacture among historic period Indians in the southeast, indicate that soapstone quarrying predates protohistorical and historic-period Indians.

Soapstone quarries typically consist of large boulders with scars or depressions left where a portion of the boulder has been removed to form a bowl. Chunks of rock, also known as blanks, were removed by chiseling and carving around an area on the parent boulder's surface until a bulge-like shape was undercut and hit loose. Blanks were then moved to nearby workshops where they were transformed into bowls through more detailed chiseling, carving, chipping, and polishing. Quarries and nearby workshops are usually characterized by considerable numbers of soapstone chips and broken-bowl fragments, as well as diabase or quartzite tools used for chiseling and carving. Contemporary habitation sites are usually located some distance away from the quarries and workshops, normally on level ground near streams or rivers. Perhaps the previously recorded archaeological site,

Site 31JK47, at the bridge across Caney Creek could have been the location of a Late Archaic camp that was associated with the quarry and workshop area around Judaculla Rock. First reported in 1964, the surface of Site JK47 has yielded diagnostic Middle Woodland period artifacts. Additional work at this site will very likely yield evidence of other earlier and later periods of occupation too. Based on archaeological evidence from elsewhere in the southeastern United States, of these, the Late Archaic and Early Woodland components are related to the quarry scars at Judaculla, whereas later Woodland, Mississippian, and historic Indian components are related to the subsequent petroglyphs. These cultural historical associations are discussed in more detail below.

Elliott (1986) has proposed a nomenclature for different types of Late Archaic quarry scars. A "stem within a depression" scar is a circular or oval stem left after the preform blank was knocked off. The depression that encircles the stem is actually the enlarged groove that was initially started around the blank. A "hollow scallop" scar is a depression without an interior stem. This type of hollow scar could represent a different technique of quarrying, possibly resembling flaking, or alternatively a technique where the stem was ultimately removed.

Two "stem within a depression" scars can be seen on the panhandle section of Judaculla Rock in a 1920 photograph. Another "stem within depression" scar occur on the upper and outer corner of a separate boulder near the bottom of the steep slope southeast from Judaculla Rock. At least three seemingly overlapping "hollow scallop" scars

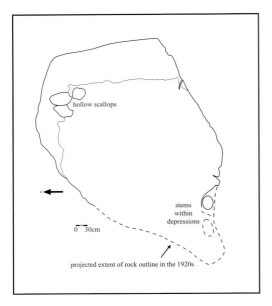

Fig 5 Soapstone quarry scars observed on Judaculla Rock

occur near the upper northeastern edge of Judaculla Rock (Fig 5).

Pecked onto these "hollow scallops" are numerous small depressions, also known as cupules, and an incised line. The occurrence of the cupules and the incised line within the scallops indicates that the cupules and line came after the quarrying of soapstone. In no instances on Judaculla Rock does a "hollow scallop" or the "stem within a depression" cut into, or truncate, a cupule or line. The placement of cupules within soapstone quarry scars instead of quarry scars cutting through cupules at Judaculla Rock is an observation that has also been made at two soapstone boulders in north central Georgia. At Sprayberry Rock in Cobb County northwest of Atlanta, a nested cross-in-circle design and cupules occur within a soapstone-bowl quarry scar (Loubser,

Hudson, and Greiner 2002). Bearing in mind that the nested cross-in-circle design is also found on Napier-style pots in the region, it is reasonable to infer via stylistic cross-dating that the engravings were made during Early Mississippian times (i.e., c.AD 1000). Knowing that the cupules are possibly contemporary and definitely later than the nested diamond, it could be that many of the cupules are more recent additions. At the Hardin Soapstone Quarry site in DeKalb County south of Atlanta, enigmatic incised designs and a cupule occur within a soapstone-bowl scar, again showing that lines and cupules postdate soapstone quarrying (Loubser 1998).

According to the stratified evidence at Judaculla Rock and at least two other prehistoric soapstone quarry sites in the southeastern United States then, cupules and lines postdate soapstone-bowl quarry scars. The rectilinear diamond, nested, concentric ring, and cross-in-circle designs on Georgia boulders (Loubser, Hudson, and Greiner 2002) and the nested-U and cross-in-circle design in the southwestern portion of Judaculla Rock are all designs that can be found on Early and Middle Mississippian-style pots. Referring to spiral designs on Hiwassee Rock in western North Carolina, Ashcraft and Moore (1998) have made similar cross-stylistic dating associations with the Mississippian period in the region.

Based on available relative dating evidence from various carefully recorded boulders in the southeastern United States (i.e., the occurrence of cupules and Mississippian-like designs on top of Late Archaic/Early Woodland soapstone-bowl scars), the petroglyphs appear to postdate the manufacture of soapstone bowls. Until evidence is found to the contrary, the chronological placement of these petroglyphs probably falls within the Late Woodland to Late Mississippian periods. Radiocarbon dates and Oxidizable Carbon Ratio dates from a dark midden that covers a cupule on the Yellow River east of Atlanta similarly fall within this window (Loubser 2005), therefore independently indicating post-Late Archaic dates for cupules and associated petroglyphs in the southeastern United States.

Wherever numerous cupules on Rheinhardt Rock in Cherokee County of Georgia and on Sprayberry Rock in nearby Cobb County co-occurs with petroglyph designs, the cupules are always part of the design or on top of the design (Loubser, Hudson, and Greiner 2002). The fact that a cupule has not yet been observed underneath a petroglyph design in northern Georgia strongly suggests that cupules are contemporary with and later than the designs, but not earlier. However, this trend is not expressed at Judaculla Rock, where cupules occur both below and on top of associated petroglyphs. A readily apparent example is the design with seven appendages near the southwestern side of the boulder (claimed by Cherokees as representing Judaculla's seven-fingered hand) (Fig 6). Here a cupule is truncated by the petroglyph (i.e., it predates the design), whereas other cupules occur within the design (i.e., they postdate the design). The same anti-symmetric stratigraphic relationship pertains between cupules and line designs in many places on the boulder. For all intents and purposes then, the lines and cupules at Judaculla Rock are broadly contemporary.

The overlap between cupules and human-like figures is also anti-symmetric;

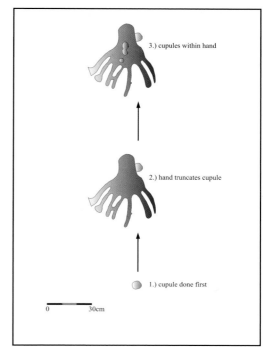

Fig 6 Example of anti-symmetric relationship between cupules and Judaculla's clawed hand

cupules are on top of figures in certain instances but are truncated by figures in others. Figures and lines are contemporary for the same reason, as are the different lines (e.g. a diagonal side-line cuts into the bold main diagonal line near the lower west central portion of the boulder). Overall then, the cupules, lines, and figures at Judaculla Rock can be viewed as "interlocked"; no motif type can be said to pre- or postdate other types. Due to the palimpsest of petroglyphs, there is no currently known way of determining a relative stratigraphy or where on the boulder the first petroglyphs were done. All that can be said at this stage of investigation is that the cupules, lines, and figure-like motifs are roughly contemporary and together these are substantially later than the soapstone quarry scars.

The concentric ring designs and nested U-shapes are stylistically similar to those found on protohistoric Cherokee ceramics. Even if future research suggests that the Cherokees did not make the petroglyphs on Judaculla Rock, which is unlikely in terms of currently available archaeological evidence in the wider region (see summary of Cherokee antiquity debate in Loubser et al. 2002), beliefs and rituals that they shared with other southeastern Indian groups in general are suggestive of remarkable antiquity and so would probably apply to Judaculla Rock. Looking at the archaeological record and the anthropogenic landscape that they created, it is reasonable to assume that Cherokee conceptions helped to shape the world that they live in, instead of merely explaining it after the fact.

Traditional Cognitive Setting

Conventional interpretations of indigenous Indian accounts concerning petroglyphs and other unusual features on the landscape automatically assume that the accounts are mere explanations of preexisting features. A somewhat extreme example of this position is Parris (1955) who states that "like all storytellers, the old Indian tale spinners of the Cherokee had their way with Judaculla." The opposite position is adopted in this article by accepting that Indian accounts concerning petroglyphs are part and parcel of deeply held shared beliefs and practices. That the network of beliefs and rituals concerning special features on the landscape is part of a wider and coherent religious system recorded and documented

by different people at different times in the American southeast alone supports the assumption that the religion of the Cherokees and their neighbors helps shape the landscape and features as we see and experience them today.

According to Native American Indian accounts across the United States and Canada, sites with petroglyphs tend to occur near or on the way to places that are believed to possess concentrated supernatural potency, particularly rapids, river pools, caves, thermal springs, mountain tops, or battlefields—all portals to the world of spirit beings or human enemies. Throughout America, Indians believe that powerful spirit beings live in the water and/or within rocks, just beyond the edge of their familiar world. Like spirit beings, mortal enemies are also located in contested regions, just beyond the boundaries of known or friendly territory. Powerful and unpredictable beings not only are seen in hallucinations and nightmares but often are actual malicious people or dangerous animals that are encountered in everyday waking life. There are repeated references in Indian ethnography to rocks and even trees (Coy 2004: 10–12) used for pecking or painting to fix and recount visions, dreams, or even specific encounters in everyday life (petroglyphs and pictographs are almost always made after individuals have returned from their "battles" in the world of altered states or world of waking consciousness). Consistent with this ethnography is the fact that petroglyph sites are often located on the pathways followed by actual hunters, warriors, and/or spirit beings (see e.g. Arsenault 2004 for the Ojibway, Francis and Loendorf 2002 for the Shoshone, Keyser 2004 for various Plains

Indians groups, and Stanley 2004 for the Winnebago).

According to Swimmer and John Axe (Mooney 1992: 430), two respected Cherokee medicine men who faithfully received and meticulously recalled many traditional Cherokee beliefs and practices, the "streams that come down from the mountains are the trails by which we reach the underworld, and the springs at their head are the doorways by which we enter it, but to do this one must fast and go to water and have one of the underground people for a guide" (Mooney 1992: 240). The "underground people," or spirit helpers, are normally the so-called Little People, but can also be giants or even animals, such as panthers and bears (Mooney 1992: 324–5). At the spring heads were vaults of solid rock, also believed to be places where the sky world (Upper World), this world, and the underworld (Lower World) meet, or a place where "the end of the sky goes down into the ground" (Mooney 1992: 440). The implication of these and other related accounts, both among the Cherokees and among Indian groups as distant as Oregon, is that those who seek visions have to fast, purify near or within water, and enter the spirit world which is viewed as being located immediately beyond the edge of the known physical world. The meeting place of the three-tiered worlds that consist of sky, land, and underground includes features such as a tree, rock, cave, mountain top, or gap in the mountain ridges.

Traveling with a spirit helper implies that the purified vision seeker submits to a supernatural power believed to be greater than him or herself (i.e., spirit helpers, or familiars, facilitate calm thoughts and controllable emotions that are of paramount importance during altered states, which by their very nature can be chaotic, unpredictable, and very frightening). It is important to note, however, that spirit beings who are the helpers of those who have control over their dreams and visions are very frightening and intimidating to those who cannot control their altered states. Among the southeastern Indians only a few seers are able to have Little People and other spirit beings work with them or even for them, whereas the majority of the population try to avoid accidental encounters with Little People from the spirit world (see e.g. Calonehuskie et al. 1989: 34; Fogelson 1982: 93; Mooney and Olbrechts 1932: 130; Swanton 1987: 774; Witthoft and Hadlock 1946: 414).

By all accounts the giant-like Judaculla appears to be a particularly powerful spirit being among the Cherokee living in the area. Judaculla is the anglicized pronunciation of the Cherokee name Tsul´kălū´ (Mooney 1992: 477), or Tsu-tla-ka-la and even Jooth-cullah in the phonetic form of the Cherokee syllabary (pamphlet produced by Cherokee Studies at Western Carolina University). According to Mooney (1992: 477) the name Tsul´kălū´ means "he has them slanting," being understood referring to the eyes of the giant. In the plural form, Judaculla is the name given to giant spirit-beings who live in the west, or land of the dead. This use of the name in a slightly different setting and the fact that Judaculla is mentioned as early as 1823 by Haywood, who spells the name as Tuli-cula, suggest that belief in this deity has some antiquity.

Like the primal shaman-like personage known as Kana´tĭ, Judaculla had dominion over game animals, many of which he hid in his underworld abode (see e.g. Mooney 1992: 262). To appease Judaculla as the "Master of the Game" and so ensure success in hunting, Cherokees included his name in their formulas. According to what late nineteenth-century Cherokees told Euro-American people working in the region (Wilburn 1952b: 24), the location of Judaculla's abode was within the Devil's Courthouse rock outcrop and the nearby Tanasee Bald (the latter is known as Tsul´kǎlū´ Tsunegûñ ĩ, or simply Tsunegûñ ĩ, in the Cherokee language). Although these high spots on the ridge line occur at the headwaters of the Tuckasegee River, they had to be approached via Judaculla's Old Fields directly below Richland Balsam at the headwaters of Caney Fork Creek (Wilburn 1952b: 25). To get to Judaculla's Old Fields, hunters had to pass Judaculla Rock, almost 10 kilometers to the west; the landmarks that bear Judaculla's name appear as transition points along a route that connected the world of living people with the world of spirits.

Judaculla's Old Fields is currently known as Judaculla Ridge, a long and prominent ridge toe slope at the point where the headwaters of Caney Fork Creek emerge from the ridge line near Richland Balsam (see the USGS Tuckasegee (NC) Topo Map). Recalling their travels through the mountains of western North Carolina, Ziegler and Grosscup (1883: 22) described this ridge as "a praire[sic]-like tract, almost level, reached by steep slopes covered with thicket of balsam and rhododendron, which seem to garrison the reputed sacred domain [of Judaculla]."

A party of Cherokee hunters once walked into the elevated Judaculla's Fields without first fasting, purifying in water, or saying the necessary prayers at Judaculla Rock. According to an account by Swimmer that is quoted in Parris (1950b: 36) the impure hunters disturbed Judaculla "who gave chase and the Indians escaped into the dense forest of spruce." The angry giant "bellowed and the heavens rumbled. From his massive bow he arrowed shafts of lightning into the forest, driving the Indians down into the valley of Caney Fork Creek and into the open. Seeing them break into the open Jutaculla [sic] made a mighty leap. He sprang from his habitat to the valley below. As he landed he stumbled and put out a hand to keep from falling. His hand pressed against a giant boulder [Judaculla Rock], steadied his massive frame [see seven-fingered hand imprint in Fig 6]. The Indians hovered at his feet, trembling in awe. Then there was a flash of blinding light, the roll of thunder, and a puff of smoke, and the Indians were gone." According to the account (Parris 1950b: 37) it "was then that Jutaculla [sic] … felt the rock. It was soft to his touch … with the nail of his right index finger he drew a sharp line across the face of the rock. The line he drew was to remind the Cherokee that death would come to all who crossed it, if first they did not make supplication and recognize his supremacy over the great hunting ground. In future years it was observed with strict respect."

The account (Parris 1950b :37) continues by stating that until "the Cherokee removal west, the hunters, chiefs, and others came annually to Jutaculla's [sic] preserve for a big hunt so they would have plenty of food through the rest of the year. They came from all sections of the mountains and encamped at Jutaculla [sic] Rock, on the safe side of the line. Each morning the priests and hunters made supplication to the god of the hunt. They asked his permission to enter his domain, which he forever granted by showing himself in the clearing on the top of the mountain and beckoning them to enter."

The mention of lighting in this account is of interest. Bartram (1955: 390), for instance, noted in the late eighteenth century that the high priests among the southeastern Indians had "communion with powerful invisible spirits, who they suppose have a share in the rule and government of human affairs, as well as the elements … and even assume the power of directing thunder and lightning." Priests and shamans seemingly exercised more effective control over powerful spirit beings, such as thunder, than ordinary people (Witthoft and Hadlock 1946: 414). Thunder and lightning were also viewed as monstrous snakes (Hudson 1978: 63; Swanton 1987: 773) that moved between the Upper and Lower Worlds (Swanton 2000: 486). According to Adair (1930: 68), southeastern Indians believed that during thunderstorms priests clashed with spirit beings. Southeastern Indians moreover believed that only those people who were struck by lightning and had recovered afterward could help others achieve success in hunting (Swanton 2000: 638).

Thunder and lightning could actually refer to physiological sensations that people experienced while they traveled to the spirit world. Prior to spirit battles with enemy sorcerers, for example, a Cherokee shaman would ask his spirit helper to "Make a clash in the very middle of my body" (Kilpatrick and Kilpatrick 1967: 134–5). Furthermore,

the voices and actions of Little People spirit helpers were commonly known to produce short, sharp claps of thunder (Fogelson 1982: 93). Reference to thunder within the bodies of priests, shamans, and sorcerers is reminiscent of the wriggling snakes, also known as thunder beings, thought to inhabit the bodies of these powerful individuals (Swanton 2000: 627). Ordinary people with sensations of lightning and snakes in their bodies would physically die if not purged (Swanton 2000: 627).

It is proposed here then that reference in the Swimmer version to thunder and lightning could be reference to sensations experienced while in altered states. In the Ziegler and Grosscup (1883: 22) version of the Old Judaculla's Fields encounter, Judaculla turned into a snake and devoured the Cherokee hunters. This account of a spirit snake that kills ordinary people contrasts with Cherokee stories of a powerful Shawnee priest who killed the fearsome Uktena snake-like being (Mooney 1992: 298–300). Visiting the spirit world is actually visiting the world of the dead; only those who have made the necessary preparations and have the necessary skills can return alive. Also, ordinary people access the spirit world only on rare occasions, and if they do so it appears that it happened because they were isolated, hungry, disoriented, and suffering from hallucinations. (See e.g. Mooney's 1992 accounts of lost hunters ultimately dying after encountering bear and panther spirit beings.) Experienced shamans and priests, however, appeared to seek out spirit beings on a regular basis, be it in dreams or in visions.

Swimmer told Mooney (1992: 337–41) about a young Cherokee woman who lived at the Cherokee town of Kanuga, on the

West Fork of the Pigeon River in Haywood County (Wilburn 1952b: 23), which is on the other side of the Balsam Mountain watershed from Judaculla Rock. The young woman appeared to be a powerful seer, as she had control over her dreams and visions and accordingly enjoyed privileged access to the world of spirit beings. It is worth noting that this woman slept in an âsĭ, or low-built sweat house, intended for fasting and transmission of sacred knowledge (Mooney 1992: 230, 462). One night Judaculla visited her while she was sleeping in the âsĭ, only to disappear with the appearance of daylight (i.e., suggesting that he appeared in her dreams while she was sleeping in the special structure, an interpretation supported in an account of Ziegler and Grosscup (1883: 23) of Judaculla appearing as a spirit in the young woman's dream). The giant hunter won the affections of the woman, considering that he brought her deer during each of his nocturnal visits. The accumulation of deer outside the âsĭ made the woman's mother curious. When the inquisitive mother transgressed and secretly looked into the âsĭ, she witnessed within the terrifying apparition of a giant, "his toes scraping the roof" (Mooney 1992: 338). Louis-Philippe's (Sturtevant 1978: 200) late eighteenth-century observation that interior beams of Cherokee lodges often had incised designs is of interest, considering that in the Swimmer story the scraping was done by a spirit being. Whatever the case might be, the irate Judaculla left Kanuga for his abode at Tanasee Bald to escape the inquisitive and unqualified mother-in-law. Soon after giving birth to Judaculla's child the woman joined her husband at Tanasee Bald. (In other Cherokee accounts, Little People spirit helpers similarly

impregnate women in their dreams; see e.g. Mooney 1992: 430.)

The woman's brother, living in a neighboring town with his wife, followed the footprints left by his sister and her giant husband. Following the trail along the headwaters of the Pigeon River up the valley to Tanasee Bald, the brother stopped at various places on the way where Judaculla, his wife, and their child rested. A second child was born at one of these resting points, the footprint petroglyphs left by the tiny feet of the two children could still be seen on the boulder in the late nineteenth century (Mooney 1992: 480). Notably, spirit-like beings, in this instance the children of a powerful female seer and her spirit helper husband Judaculla, have made the petroglyphs. The boulder is still known "where their tracks are this way," or Datsu´nălâsgûñ ĭ, in the Cherokee language.

Although the petroglyphs both at this site and at Judaculla Rock were made by spirit beings, the circumstances appear reversed. Whereas at the Datsu´nălâsgûñ ĭ petroglyph site small children left footprints while slowly ascending the mountain to the southwest, at Judaculla Rock the giant adult left a handprint while quickly descending the mountain in a northwesterly direction. The connotation of this opposition is worth further investigation. Another parallel is that the resting points from Kanuga via Datsu´nălâsgûñ ĭ on the way to Tanasee Bald are reminiscent of the stopover points from Cullowhee via Judaculla Rock to Tanasee Bald. This suggests that trails along drainages connected various Cherokee "Out Towns" with Tanasee Bald. Moreover, in Cherokee thought the Pigeon River to the northeast of Tanasee Bald and the Caney Fork Creek to the northwest of the same peak each probably represented a "Long Man, a giant with its head in … the mountains and his foot far down in the lowland, speaking in murmurs only a shaman can understand" (Mooney 1982: 30).

After following the upper reaches of the Pigeon River, the woman's brother finally reached Tanasee Bald where "he heard the sound of a drum and voices, as if people were dancing inside the mountain. Soon he came to a cave like a doorway in the side of the mountain, but the rock was so steep and smooth that he could not climb up to it, but could only just look over the edge and see the heads and shoulders of a great many people dancing inside. He saw his sister dancing among them and called to her to come out. She turned when she heard him … finding no trouble to climb down the rock, and leading her two little children by hand … and he could never see her husband" (Mooney 1992: 339–40). This account strongly suggests that while the woman and her children had the requisite powers to enter and exit the spirit world at will, her brother was not quite up to it; at best he was only able to hear Judaculla's voice.

Like the woman's brother, the people from Kanuga town wished to talk to and see Judaculla, bearing in mind that the "Master of the Game" owned and could supply them with all the game in the mountains. However, in order to gain Judaculla's favor Kanuga's inhabitants had to enter their townhouse and fast for seven days. The people failed to fast for the full seven days and were only able to hear thunder and see lightning in the direction of Tanasee Bald.

In another version of the Judaculla story recorded by Haywood (Mooney 1992:

478), the thunder and lightning shook the ground down in the valley so violently that the townhouse was turned into a mound. Interestingly a mound occurs at the important valley-bottom towns Kanuga and Cullowhee. One possible meaning of Cullowhee could be "giant place." In the Cherokee language, the marker –wi or –i denotes geographic place. The area would accordingly become jooth-cullah-wee. Over time, and with the settlement of Euro-Americans, the unaccented first syllable was likely dropped and the result is cullah-wee (pamphlet produced by Cherokee Studies at Western Carolina University). If this is indeed the case then the Cherokee town at Cullowhee was more intimately linked with Judaculla Rock and the mountain balds beyond than previously thought.

In addition to Judaculla Rock, Cullowhee town, Kanuga town, Datsu´nălâsgûñ´ĩ, Devil's Courthouse, Tanasee Bald, and Judaculla Old Field that feature in accounts of the "Master of the Game," there are two more places in the Balsam Mountain region that refer to Judaculla by name (Fig 7). The first is Judaculla Mountain, a semi-isolated ridge northeast of the modern town Sylva (Wilburn 1952b: 23, 26). The second is Tsulâ´sinûn´yĭ, or "where the footprint is," on the Tuckasegee River, roughly a mile above Deep Creek (Mooney 1992: 409). At Tsulâ´sinûn´yĭ the footprints of Judaculla and a deer could be seen on a petroglyph boulder until railroad construction destroyed the boulder in the late nineteenth century (ibid. 410). If Mooney's description of the petroglyph boulder is correct, then it must have been near the floodplain of Kadua town (one of the "seven mother towns" of the Cherokee people living in the Tuckasegee

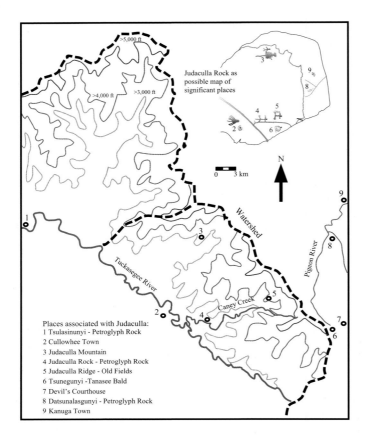

Fig 7 Judaculla's world on the Balsam Mountains and on the boulder

Places associated with Judaculla:
1 Tsulasinunyi - Petroglyph Rock
2 Cullowhee Town
3 Judaculla Mountain
4 Judaculla Rock - Petroglyph Rock
5 Judaculla Ridge - Old Fields
6 Tsunegunyi -Tanasee Bald
7 Devil's Courthouse
8 Datsunalasgunyi - Petroglyph Rock
9 Kanuga Town

River valley and a prominent political and religious center). More place names and features in the region are very likely related to Judaculla; these either are forgotten or still have to be found or are kept secret. Interestingly, Mooney (1992: 431) mentions that certain stories are held so sacred among the Cherokees that any person who wishes to hear a story from a knowledgeable elder must first purify by fasting and "going to water" in a running stream at daybreak. It could very well be, then, that particularly potent stories and places associated with Judaculla are simply not mentioned to "polluted" and unprepared outsiders.

Judging from the occurrence of various Judaculla place-names in the Balsam Mountains north and east of Judaculla Rock (Wilburn 1952b), this "Master of the Game" must have featured prominently in the lives of Cherokees of the area. When looking at the slanted Judaculla Rock and the prominent diagonal lines that run across its southwestern side, the boulder may tantalizingly be a scale-model of Judaculla's world. The southeastern Indians, including the Cherokees, are known to have drawn stylized maps on various media, ranging from sand and rocks through tree bark to animal hides (see e.g. Hammett 1997). The orientation of the main bold diagonal line on the north–south-oriented Judaculla Rock corresponds with the orientation of the Tuckasegee River, whereas the orientation of the secondary diagonal line corresponds with that of Caney Fork Creek (see Fig 7). If this is indeed the case then the location of other prominent landscape features and even towns can be located on the boulder.

Various mountaintop balds in western North Carolina were believed to contain the towns and town houses of spirit beings. Ordinary Cherokees believed that the spirit beings living within these underground towns could "see you wherever you go and are with you in all your dances, but you cannot see us unless you fast" (Mooney 1992: 342). The interiors of all the balds occupied by spirit beings were thought to be the same; great doors within the cliff faces would open up for those who could fast for seven days, revealing towns of the spirit beings, or mountain people, within. These underworld towns had "houses ranged in two long rows from east to west. The mountain people lived in the houses on the south side … there was another town, of a different people, above them in the same mountain, and still farther above, at the very top, lived … the Thunders" (Mooney 1992: 342).

In light of the ethnographic information provided above it could be that Judaculla Rock is a three-dimensional map of the Balsam Mountains. Each "dot-within-outline" design (i.e., one or more cupules encircled by a line or a number of intersecting lines (Fig 8)) could represent a house (outline) with a fire-place and/or pits (dots). The arrangement of these designs from east to west on Judaculla Rock could reflect the above-quoted "houses ranged in two long

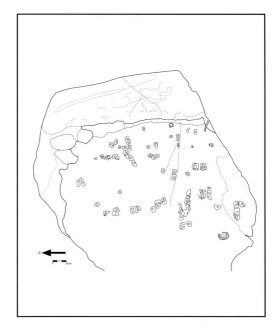

Fig 8 "Dot-within-outline" motifs observed on Judaculla Rock

rows from east to west" (Mooney 1992: 342). While some lines could represent trails that divide or connect settlements, the two most prominent diagonal lines lower down the boulder could represent the Tuckasegee River and Caney Fork Creek as already discussed.

The ritual importance of rivers and creeks is well documented among various southeastern Indian groups. For the Cherokee, Mooney (1992: 341) notes that during "every important ceremony—whether connected with … hunting…—contains a prayer to the "Long Person," the formalistic name … for the river." Other features where prayers were conducted included rocks, mountains, trees, river reeds, and central fires within houses and townhouses (Mooney 1992: 341–2). Each of these features is thought to be the residence of a spirit being, so portrayals of these features are likely to contain human attributes. For instance, a being known as Whirlwind abides in the evergreen tops of cedars, and this being has humanlike attributes. Tantalizingly, the carved tree-like motif on the northwestern side of Judaculla Rock could represent a cedar, complete with a human-head-like appendage at its top. (Additional discussion concerning the provisional identification of carved motifs and figures on Judaculla Rock appear under "Picture Maps and Altered States of Consciousness" below.)

Overall then, it could be argued that Judaculla Rock is a highly stylized scale-model of the surrounding sacred landscape with its mountains, rivers, red cedars, villages, and spirit beings. In a sense the boulder depicts things that are invisible to the everyday awake person; only an Indian dreaming or experiencing a related "out-of-body" mental state could claim to have had a bird's-eye view of the Balsam Mountains and its rivers. (An oblique view of this landscape can perhaps be had by standing at the headwaters of drainages, especially on the higher ridgelines and balds of the Balsam Mountains.) Moreover, the spirit beings and their spirit villages were believed to occur underground; only through prolonged fasting, prayer, and altered states of consciousness could a privileged few people enter this underworld. In short, the petroglyphs on Judaculla Rock reveal what is normally concealed from the gaze of ordinary people; the rock art has made the invisible visible, or, intangible inner mental constructs have been turned outward on a tangible rock. Beliefs about the landscape and the spirit beings normally concealed within are given outward expression in the petroglyphs; Judaculla Rock is in effect a nexus between the mindscape and the landscape of the Cherokee people who once inhabited the Caney Fork Creek and Tuckasegee River valleys.

But as in the case of most of Native American Indian culture, the sacred and the profane could reside at one and the same location, depending on the event or the time of year (see e.g. Walker 1991). Parris (1950a) writes that the Cherokee "annually gathered in the Fall for a grand hunt and to lay up food for the Winter. They came from throughout the mountains to Jutaculla [sic] Rock. And there, every morning during the annual encampment, they would gather and make supplication to Jutaculla [sic], asking his permission to cross into his domain for the annual hunt."

It is perhaps also to be expected that Judaculla Rock could be used as a convenient "picture-map" to plan or even commemorate and delineate military victories against neighboring groups, such as Muskogee-speaking Creeks or Siouan-speaking Catawba Indians (see e.g. James Blythe, a Cherokee Indian being quoted in a Special Report of the *Asheville Citizen* 1937; Wilburn 1952a: 20–1; Wilburn 1954). Being located near the eastern edge of the "Out Towns," Judaculla Rock was not only on the boundary between the world of living people and the world of spirit beings, but also on that between the world of cultivated plants and the world of hunted animals, and between the world of Iroquoian-speaking Cherokees and the worlds of neighboring linguistic groups.

At certain times these binary sets of worlds became intertwined, if not confused. For example, it is telling that when the "seer" woman left Kanuga town to join her spirit-being husband Judaculla within Tanasee Bald, "her supposed abduction caused great excitement among her people … they made war upon the neighboring tribes in the hope of finding the place of her concealment. Grieved because of so much bloodshed … she appeared unto the chiefs in a dream, and charged them to meet the spirits of the hunting ground with fear and reference" (Ziegler and Grosscup 1883: 22). Tales of spiritual encounters during altered states of consciousness and tales of actual events during waking consciousness are almost certainly both expressed at Judaculla Rock; to claim that the petroglyph and rock have only a single meaning would go against the universal understanding that places have multiple meanings and significances, depending on the relevant state of consciousness that is being expressed at any given time or occasion.

Wilburn (1954) believes that Judaculla Rock is a picture map of the Battle of Taliwa, fought in the year 1755. The battle was fought between the Cherokees and Creeks near the town of Canton in Georgia. After this battle the victorious Cherokee settled into the formerly Creek-occupied territory of northwestern Georgia and northeastern Alabama. The Cherokees lived in the area, centered on their capital town New Echota, until their final removal to Oklahoma by 1838. According to Wilburn, lines and figures on Judaculla Rock depict battle positions and important warrior chiefs.

Dan Tomkins, editor of the *Jackson County Journal*, was told many years ago that Judaculla Rock is a Cherokee record of a treaty between them and Euro-Americans in 1793 (Special Report 1937). The straight diagonal line near the southwestern edge of the boulder is a depiction of the Meigs and Freeman line, on the east of which the Euro-Americans had their land and on the west the Cherokees.

It is indeed conceivable that the petroglyphs were reinterpreted in the historic period to commemorate important victories and treaties. But it should also be remembered that the Cherokees continued to pay homage to Judaculla at his boulder, even after their removal to Oklahoma in 1838 (see e.g. Wilburn 1954). It appears then that the boulder served multiple purposes in historic times, depending on the time of year and on the occasion.

Additional Comments on Picture Maps and Altered States of Consciousness

The location of at least some motifs on the boulder can be interpreted in terms of published Judaculla stories and place-names. If it is accepted that the boulder is indeed a three-dimensional picture map of the upper Tuckasegee River and Caney Fork Creek drainages and the western slopes of the Balsam Mountains, then the location of certain motifs are suggestive of their identity. What has to be realized from studying Indian maps on deerskin, for example, is that their maps are not drawn to scale; it is the spatial relationship between places and people that are correct. (For example, a deerskin map drawn by a Catawba chief in the late eighteenth century shows the correct order and direction of major Indian settlements, indicated as circles, in relation to

Time and Mind　　Volume 2—Issue 3—November 2009, pp. 287–312

Charlestown harbor, indicated as a grid with a sailing-ship nearby, even though any sense of scale is absent: see Hammett 1997: 196.) Another common characteristic of Indian maps is that whereas some features, such as settlements, are shown as if they are viewed from above, other features, such as certain houses or people, are shown as if they are viewed from the side (hence the term "picture map"). Furthermore, Indian maps, like the Catawba map (Hammett 1997) and like the biographic pictographs and ledger drawings of the Plains Indians (see e.g. Keyser 2004), almost always include a narrative component by adding human figures. Similar-looking figures that are depicted more than once on the same canvas are actually one and the same person who is engaged in different activities. (In the sequential art of comic strips, movement is normally depicted by placing the same figure in a series of distinct cells.) Moreover, on deerskin maps of southeastern Indians, Hammett (1997: 197) has identified the following three recurring features: 1) patches (towns); 2) corridors (trails and rivers), and 3) surrounding matrix (figures and empty spaces). It is proposed here, as a working hypothesis, that the characteristics and conventions expressed on deerskin maps are also apparent on Judaculla Rock.

Between the hypothesized headwaters of the Tuckasegee River and Caney Fork Creek on Judaculla Rock could be a side-on representation of Judaculla's dome-shaped town house within Tanasee Bald and/or Devil's Courthouse (Fig 9). Cherokees describe their town houses as dome-shaped when viewed from the side (see e.g. Mooney 1992: 336). When viewed from above the same town houses look like concentric rings

(e.g. Mooney 1992: 347). It is suggested that the concentric ring design on Judaculla Rock could represent the townhouse underneath the mound at Cullowhee Town, which is located northwest of the confluence of Caney Fork Creek and the Tuckasegee River. The seven-fingered handprint could somehow be associated with Buzzard's Roost Hill immediately to the north of the Cullowhee Mound (although there is as yet no ethnographic account to support this speculative association). The two similar-looking figures carved immediately north of the hypothesized Caney Fork Creek on Judaculla Rock could be depictions of the actual Giant. The eastern figure's location corresponds with Judaculla's Old Fields, whereas the western figure's location immediately next to the proposed Caney Fork Creek could be Judaculla Rock. Viewed together the paired figures are conceivably a narration of Judaculla's famed leap.

Near the northwestern edge of Judaculla Rock is a depiction of a tree-like motif. The occurrence of a headlike appendage on the tip of the treelike motif recalls the Cherokee story of a sorcerer's severed head that was tied to the top of a cedar tree (Mooney 1992: 421). Diagonally upslope and slightly northeast from this treelike motif is a motif that resembles the seedpod, or ovary, of a datura plant (*Datura stramonium*) as if it were cut through across its length (i.e., a longitudinal-section view). Although the stem of the motif is too long for that of a datura plant, it is interesting how the bottom of the motif abuts a cracked edge of a flake on the boulder's surface, as if it is coming out of the boulder. Two engraved figures touch this datura-like motif.

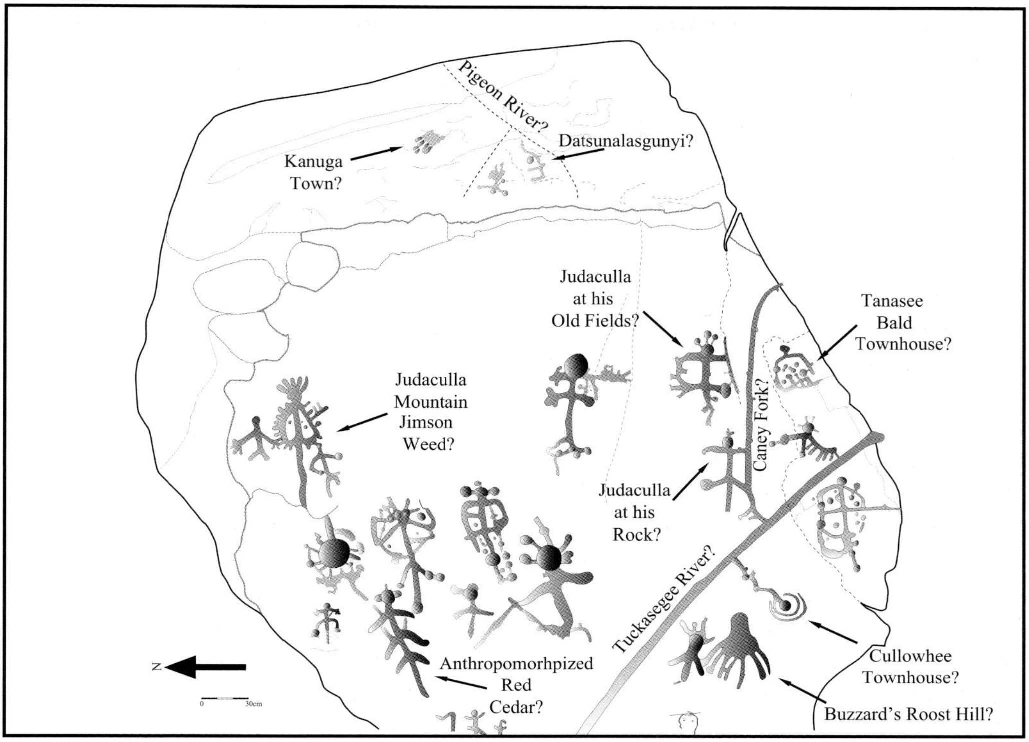

Fig 9 Possible identifications of motifs on Judaculla Rock as a picture map

Datura stramonium, also known as jimsonweed, is a common weed in the Nightshade Family. It contains tropane alkaloids that are sometimes used as a hallucinogen. Tropane alkaloids are poisonous but in small doses are accompanied by delirium with visual and auditory hallucinations. The effects of datura have been described as a living dream: consciousness falls in and out, people who don't exist or are miles away are conversed with. The effects can last for days. Tropane alkaloids are some of the few substances which cause true hallucinations that cannot be distinguished from reality. It may be described as a "real" trance when a user under the effect can be awake but completely disconnected from his immediate environment. In this case, the user would ignore most stimuli and respond to unreal ones. This is unlike psilocybin or LSD, which only cause sensory distortions. Users who have written reports on experiences with this plant have described those experiences as unpleasant and often terrifying.

Datura is currently found in cultivated and disturbed areas throughout the southeastern United States, although its natural habitat is typically within rocky crevices. The prehistoric distribution of datura in the southeastern United States woodlands has not been determined with any degree of certainty. Even though datura seeds are difficult to identify, Johannessen (1993: 199) describes an excavated ritual structure in the American Bottom area of the Mississippi Valley that "contained a high percentage of red cedar and seeds of the hallucinogen jimsonweed (*Datura stramonium*)." The association of datura and red cedar within a special-purpose house structure is of interest here, as both have ritual connotations and the interiors of both plants are colored red. The tantalizing question that the identification of possible datura at Judaculla Rock raises is its use by proto- and prehistoric peoples who once lived in the area. The terrifying stories associated with the Judaculla giant-being can, for example, be explained by the imbibing of prepared jimsonweed. (Native Californian Indians prepared datura by soaking in water the plant's roasted seeds or roasted ground roots: Dave Whitley, personal communication.) It has been documented that Cherokees smoked wild tobacco leaves, or *Nicotiana rustica*, for mind-altering purposes (see e.g. Mooney 1992: 439), but datura is not mentioned. Until independent evidence is found in the ethnographic or archaeological record, the identification of jimsonweed on Judaculla Rock must remain tentative, in a large part due to the stylized execution of the motif.

From a Western materialist and uniformitarian perspective it is reasonable to infer that humans and not actual spirit beings or natural processes carved the various petroglyphs, both at Judaculla Rock and at other rocks mentioned in the Judaculla-related stories. It is proposed here, based on ethnography elsewhere in the Americas and beyond (see for example the 1494 and 1496 accounts of Taíno Indian rock art by Fray Ramón Pané in Arrom 1999), that human beings produced the petroglyphs while in an alert, everyday, and awake state of consciousness. Nonetheless, the petroglyphs do recount visions and experiences of altered states, such as dreams and deep trance. (This is described, for example, by Pané in the late fifteenth century, which is the oldest account of rock-art production in the New World (Arrom 1999: 26.) Even if the engraver did not personally experience the actual altered states, the Judaculla stories ultimately recall encounters with imagined spirit beings in dreams and trance visions. In the final analysis it is perhaps reasonable to conclude that what has been engraved on the boulder can be traced back to altered-state experiences of certain seers, even though the experiences are recounted and carved into stone during times of mental tranquility.

The numerous cupules found on Judaculla Rock could also relate to altered states. Twentieth-century accounts collected from southeastern Indians show that ordinary people still encounter spirit beings at isolated locations where cupules are to be found. At the age of six a Muskogee Creek was directed by an invisible voice to "a big flat rock" on the edge of a river to begin his initiations into the world of shamans (Lewis and Jordan 2002: 49). In the middle of the rock was a meticulously pecked cupule and within the cupule were root medicines. After the boy chewed some of the root, the rock made a loud cracking sound like thunder that scared the boy away. In a related story a Natchez told Swanton (2000: 497) that while out hunting he heard a voice. After a while he saw the Little Person who was doing the talking. This apparition directed him to a stone cupule filled with medicine that would help him find deer. After drinking the medicine he successfully killed a deer. In these accounts the altered state of consciousness experienced by the Natchez adult was more intense than that of the young Muskogee initiate: whereas the Muskogee boy only had a supposedly aural hallucination, the Natchez man experienced a visual hallucination of a Little Person as well.

Cupules, similar to the ones on Judaculla Rock, occur on a concentration of four big round boulders on the eastern bank of Caney Fork Creek (labeled Site 31JK464). Whereas most cupules occur on top of the boulders, some are also visible on the vertical sides. The vertically placed cupules strongly suggest that they were not necessarily hollows to process nuts or to grind corn. Boulders with cupules normally occur near rivers or creeks, mostly near sites that contain Woodland- or Mississippian-period ceramics (Loubser 2005). Site 31JK464 seems to fit this pattern, as it is immediately east of the known Woodland-period Site 31JK47.

Unlike boulders with cupules only that are located on the edge of habitation sites, boulders with engraved motifs and cupules, such as Judaculla Rock, typically occur in more isolated locations, far away from any habitation sites. It is this peripheral placement on the landscape that reflects the peripheral locales where altered states of consciousness were experienced among historic-period southeastern Indians. Unlike the centrality of the southern African San fire-place in terms of everyday life and the trance dance (see e.g. Lewis-Williams and Pearce 2004), trance experience was a peripheral activity among the southeastern Indians, both in terms of everyday life and its occurrence on the landscape.

Acknowledgements
Kenneth Westmoreland, Jackson County Manager, is thanked for his support throughout the course of the project. The United States Forest Service is acknowledged for supporting the North Carolina Rock Art Survey by donating the time and office space of Scott Ashcraft and Rodney Snedeker. Douglas Frink, Scott Ashcraft, and Lorie Hanson are thanked for volunteering their time and advice, such as helping to excavate the deposit immediately west of Judaculla Rock and reading drafts of this report. David Dyson graciously helped out with equipment. Gratitude is due to Jerry Parker, owner of the property adjacent to the Judaculla Rock parcel, for his friendly support and supply of useful information. Al Webster Jr. is thanked for setting up the generator and halogen lamps at night and for helping in many other ways during the day, including relocating the cupule site on Caney Fork Creek. The valuable academic input of Tom Hatley, Anne Rogers, and Steve Yurkovich at Western Carolina University is much appreciated. Linda Hall, the western North Carolina archaeologist for the State Historic Preservation Office, is thanked for her site visit. Brett Riggs, Lee Newsom, and Dave Whitley freely shared their specialist knowledge. The Caney Fork Community's volunteer work on the site's infrastructure is acknowledged. Deborah

Kerzhner is thanked for helping out with the graphics.

References

Adair, J., 1930. *Adair's History of the American Indians*, ed. S.C. Williams. New York: Promontory Press.

Arrom, J.J., 1999. *An Account of the Antiquities of the Indians of Fray Ramón Pané, Chronicles of the New World Encounter*, Durham, NC: Duke University Press.

Arsenault, D., 2004. "Analyzing and Dating the Nisula Site, Québec." in C. Diaz-Granados and J.R. Duncan (eds), *The Rock-Art of Eastern North America: Capturing Images and Insights*. Tuscaloosa, AL: University of Alabama Press, pp. 344–60.

Ashcraft, A.S. and Moore, D., 1998. "Native American Rock Art in Western North Carolina." in D.G. Moore and A.S. Ashcraft (eds), *Collected Papers on the Archaeology of Western North Carolina*. Cherokee: Fall Meeting of the North Carolina Archaeological Society, pp. 59–88.

Bartram, W., 1955. *Travels of William Bartram*, ed. M. Van Doren. New York: Dover.

Brown, P.M., 1985. *Geologic Map of North Carolina*. Raleigh, NC: North Carolina Geological Survey.

Calonehuskie, L., Jackson, G., and Davis, E., 1989. "Fading Voices." *Journal of Cherokee Studies* 11:1–85.

Coy, F.E., 2004. "Native American Dendroglyphs of the Eastern Woodlands." in C. Diaz-Granados and J.R. Duncan (eds), *The Rock-Art of Eastern North America: Capturing Images and Insights*. Tuscaloosa, AL: University of Alabama Press, pp. 3–18.

Dickens, R. and Carnes, L., 1983. "Preliminary Investigations at Soapstone Ridge in DeKalb County, Georgia." *Southeastern Archaeological Conference Bulletin* 20 and 21: 81–97.

Elliott, D.T., 1986. *The Live Oak Soapstone Quarry, DeKalb County, Georgia*. Atlanta: Garrow and Associates.

Fogelson, R.D., 1982. "Cherokee Little People Reconsidered." *Journal of Cherokee Studies* 7(2): 92–98.

Francis, J.E. and Loendorf, L.L., 2002. *Ancient Visions: Petroglyphs and Pictographs from the Wind River and Bighorn Country, Wyoming and Montana*. Salt Lake City, UT: University of Utah Press.

Hammett, J.E., 1997. "Interregional Patterns of Land Use and Plant Management in Native North America." in K.J. Gremillion (ed.), *People, Plant, and Landscape Studies in Paleoethnobotony*. Tuscaloosa, AL: University of Alabama Press, pp. 195–216.

Hudson, C., 1978. *The Southeastern Indians*. Knoxville, TN: University of Tennessee Press.

Johannessen, S., 1993. "Food, Dishes, and Society in the Mississippi Valley." in C. M. Scarry (ed.), *Foraging and Farming in the Eastern Woodlands*. Gainesville, FL: University Press of Florida, pp. 182–205.

Keyser, J.D. 2004. *Art of the Warrior: Rock Art of the American Plains*. Salt Lake City, UT: University of Utah Press.

Kilpatrick, J.F. and Kilpatrick, A.G., 1967. *Run Towards the Nightland: Magic of the Oklahoma Cherokees*. Dallas, TX: Southern Methodist University Press.

Lewis, D. and Jordan A.T., 2002. *Creek Indian Medicine Ways: The Enduring Power of Muskoke Religion*. Albuquerque, NM: University of New Mexico Press.

Lewis-Williams, J.D. and Pearce, D.G., 2004. *San Spirituality: Roots, Expression, and Social Consequences*. Walnut Creek, CA: AltaMira Press.

Loubser, J.H.N., 1998. *Field Survey of Cove Lake Estates, Land Lot 20, DeKalb County, Georgia*. Atlanta, GA: New South Associates.

Loubser, J.H.N., 2005. "In Small Cupules Forgotten: Rock Markings, Archaeology, and Ethnography in the Deep South." in L.L. Loendorf, C.C. Chippindale, and D.S. Whitley (eds), *Discovering North American Rock Art*. Tucson, AZ: University of Arizona Press, pp. 131–60.

Loubser, J. and Frink, D., 2008. *Heritage Resource Conservation Plan for Judaculla Rock, State Archaeological Site 31JK3, North Carolina*. Sylva: Stratum Unlimited.

Loubser, J., Hudson, T., and Greiner, T., 2002. "The Recent Recording of Petroglyphs in Georgia." *The Profile* 117: 3–5.

Loubser, J., Raymer, L., Meader, J., and Joseph, J., 2002. *A Traditional Cultural Study of New Echota, the First Cherokee National Capital from 1825–1838, Gordon County, Georgia*. Atlanta, GA: New South Associates.

Mooney, J., 1982. "The Cherokee River Cult." *Journal of Cherokee Studies* 17: 30–6.

Mooney, J., 1992. *James Mooney's History, Myths, and Sacred Formulas of the Cherokees*. Asheville: Historical Images.

Mooney, J. and Olbrechts, F.M., 1932. "The Swimmer Manuscript: Cherokee Sacred Formulas and Medicinal Prescriptions." *Bureau of American Ethnology Bulletin* 99.

Parris, J., 1950a. "Mythical Jutaculla: The Paul Bunyan of his Race." *Durham Evening Herald*, May 29.

Parris, J., 1950b. *The Cherokee Story*. Asheville: Stephens Press.

Parris, J., 1955. "Mysterious Judaculla Rock: Scientist Seeks to Break Secret of Message Carved upon Huge Stone in Jackson County." *Asheville Citizen-Times*, February 6.

Pratt, J.H. and Lewis, J.V., 1905. "Corundum and the Peridotites of Western North Carolina." *NC Geological Survey* 1: 464.

Sassaman, K.E., 1997. "Refining Soapstone Vessel Chronology in the Southeast." *Early Georgia* 25(1): 1–20.

Special Report. 1937. "Jutaculla Rock is One of Ancient Mysteries of Western North Carolina: Indian Legends Center around Rude Carvings, Meaning of Inscription is Lost in Antiquity is Near Sylva." *Asheville Citizen*. October 3.

Stanley, L.A. 2004. "Ratcliffe Sacred Rock and Seven Sacred Stones." in C. Diaz-Granados and J.R.

Duncan (eds), *The Rock-Art of Eastern North America: Capturing Images and Insights*. Tuscaloosa, AL: University of Alabama Press, pp. 19–41.

Sturtevant, W.C., 1978. "Louis-Philippe on Cherokee Architecture and Clothing in 1797." *Journal of Cherokee Studies* 3(8): 198–205.

Swanton, J.R., 1987. *The Indians of the Southeastern United States*. Washington, DC: Smithsonian Institution Press.

Swanton, J.R., 2000. *Creek Religion and Medicine*. Lincoln, NE: University of Nebraska Press.

Wagner, M.J., 1996. "Written in Stone: An Overview of the Rock Art of Illinois." in C.H. Faulkner (ed.), *Rock Art of the Eastern Woodlands*. San Miguel: American Rock Art Research Association, Occasional Paper No. 2, pp. 47–80.

Walker, D.E., 1991. "Protection of American Indian Sacred Geography." in C. Vecsey (ed.), *Handbook of American Indian Religious Freedom*. New York: Crossroad Publishing, pp. 100–15.

Wilburn, H.C., 1952a. "Judaculla Rock." *Southern Indian Studies* 4: 19–22.

Wilburn, H.C., 1952b. "Judaculla Place-Names and the Judaculla Tales." *Southern Indian Studies* 4: 23–6.

Wilburn, H.C., 1954. "Judaculla Rock May be Map of Big Indian Battle, Study made of Notable WNC Relic." *Asheville Citizen-Times*, July 18.

Witthoft, J. and Hadlock, W.S., 1946. Cherokee-Iroquois Little People. *Journal of American Folklore* 59: 413–22.

Ziegler, W.G. and Grosscup, B.S., 1883. *The Heart of the Alleghanies, or Western Carolina*. Raleigh, NC: Alfred Williams and Company.

Time and Mind:
The Journal of
Archaeology,
Consciousness
and Culture

Volume 2—Issue 3
November 2009
pp. 313–332

DOI:
10.2752/175169609X12464529903137

Modern Druidry and Earth Mysteries

Ronald Hutton

Ronald Hutton is Professor of History at Bristol University,
and the author of thirteen books on different aspects
of the past and of attitudes to it, most concerned with
Britain but some venturing as far as America and Siberia.
R.Hutton@bristol.ac.uk

Abstract
The history of "alternative" forms of spirituality in
modern Britain is now starting to be written, although
the ventures into it to date have the character of
pioneering works. This article compares two of the most
prominent such forms of spirituality in twentieth-century
England, both characterized by a close relationship
with prehistoric monuments: Druidry and the Earth
Mysteries movement. It formulates the main distinguishing
features of the former and then charts the development
of the latter, viewing it, like the former, primarily as a
form of religious and cultural expression. This exercise
permits a systematic comparison of the two, and also
an examination of their relationship with orthodox
archaeology and history. In the process, it is hoped not
only to be able to gain new insights into the nature of
twentieth-century British counter-cultures, but into the
nature of modern British culture as a whole.

Keywords: Druids, Earth Mysteries, prehistory,
archaeology, religious studies, modernity, radical culture

Introduction
The history of forms of "alternative" spirituality in the
twentieth century—those movements which developed
in self-conscious opposition to established religions and
cultural norms—is only just beginning to be written. Two
of those forms shared with others the general criteria of
such spirituality, stated above, but were distinguished by the
particular intensity with which they identified themselves

with the ancient British past. One was modern English Druidry, which as a form of alternative spirituality was born in the years between 1912 and 1918 with the development of a society called the Universal Bond. This endures to the present day, and gave birth from 1938 onward to a series of other orders which embodied its basic principles while developing and modifying them. Some initial work has been carried out into its history by Adam Stout and myself (Stout 2005 and 2008; 113–54; Hutton 2007: 172–93, 2009: 348–410). It attracted public attention in particular because of its midsummer rites at Stonehenge, and its members identified themselves with the ancient Druids, as figures of learning and wisdom, who were presumed to have enjoyed both a close understanding of the natural world and a spiritual relationship with it.

The other movement was that of the Earth Mysteries, which was more loosely organised and defined; indeed, the unifying term for it was not adopted until 1974. If it had any centrally important focus of the sort provided by the Universal Bond for modern Druidry, this was represented in the early twentieth century by a society, the Straight Track Club, and later in the century by a journal, *The Ley Hunter*. What united it was a sense of the numinous qualities of prehistoric sites, which to most members reflected a benevolent ancient spiritual tradition linked to forces inherent in the earth itself. Most believed that this tradition had originated in the very remote past of humanity and persisted until relatively recent times, and was embodied in landscape features and monuments not generally recognized by mainstream

archaeologists. The Earth Mysteries have also begun to be given a history, by Paul Screeton, Paul Devereux, Nigel Pennick, Bob Trubshaw, and (again) Adam Stout (Screeton 1984–5; Pennick and Devereux 1989: 1–38; Devereux 1994: 1–37; Trubshaw 2005: 79–108; Stout 2006 and 2008: 155–233). So how do the two now seem to compare, and what was the relationship between them?

Modern Druidry

It seems best to begin by summarizing what is now known of the beliefs of the Universal Bond and the Druidic groups that hived off from it. This is partly because those groups were more compact than Earth Mysteries researchers or devotees, and had a more unitary ideology, but also because the present author has written extensively of them elsewhere, in the works cited above. It is proposed here to summarize their main features, as they manifested between the 1910s and the 1980s, one by one. The rest of this article can then be devoted to introducing new material concerning Earth Mysteries, and then the two movements can be systematically compared. A first notable characteristic of modern English spiritual Druidry was that it was distinctively twentieth-century. Druid societies had existed in England continuously since 1781, but were social and insurance clubs rather than being concerned primarily with spirituality in the manner of the Universal Bond. In Wales, certainly, modern Druidry had been turned into a form of religion by the 1840s, and some of the publications of Welsh Druids were to have an influence on the English movement, but there was no direct connection between the two. A second characteristic of modern English Druids was their treatment of prehistoric sites, especially megalithic monuments, as living sacred places and settings for revived worship. A corollary of this was their tendency to reject the practice of mainstream European scholars, since the mid-nineteenth century, to divide up prehistory into different ages, associated with distinct technologies, monuments, religions, and (for most such commentators) races. The Druids, instead, viewed prehistory as a continuum of belief and practice, which could all be associated with the ancient priests whose name they had taken and which transformed into a particularly admirable and distinctive form of British Christianity at the end of the pagan era.

This attitude was bound up with a fourth and a fifth feature of their ideology. The former was that in many respects their treatment of prehistory was based firmly on an older scholarly orthodoxy, which had prevailed until the middle of the nineteenth century. Introduced above all by William Stukeley in the 1740s, this had likewise classed most prehistoric monuments in the British Isles as the products of a common culture—and religion—over which the Druids had presided. It did so because those monuments were recognized by Stukeley, correctly, as pre-Roman, and because the first priesthood that the earliest historical sources identified in these islands happened to be the Druids. Their twentieth-century counterparts chose to uphold this earlier interpretation of antiquity against the new system introduced by Victorian intellectuals; and indeed that new system was still becoming familiar to the general public in

the early twentieth century and was not generally accepted by it until the 1960s. This attitude to the past was closely linked to the fifth notable feature of modern English Druidry: that in many ways it clung to a Biblical view of humanity and its development which had been overthrown by those same Victorian savants who had divided prehistory into separate ages. That view depended on the idea of an original, worldwide religion which had been revealed to the ancestors of the human race by a wise and good god, and which had kept humans in harmony with that deity, and so with each other and all the rest of his creation. In the Biblical story, the divine gift of free will had led humanity into wickedness, by which the original good religion and society had become corrupted, causing people to fall into discord with their creator and his world, and so with each other. All manner of sufferings, and crimes against humanity and the natural order of being, had resulted. Built into modern English Druidry was the concept of such a fall from original divine grace and human happiness. It led both to a fear that too great a disharmony with the creator and with the world would result in the utter destruction of our species and to a hope that by regaining a knowledge and practice of the old pristine faith, we might instead enter into a new age of peace, harmony and general wellbeing.

Another aspect of modern Druidic ideology, comparatively slight but still significant, was its acceptance at times of the modern myth of Atlantis, as developed in the United States in the 1880s. This was essentially a post-Christian reworking of Noah's Flood, cutting the latter off from its Biblical and Near Eastern roots and resetting the scene of it (conveniently for English speakers) between Britain and North America. The same basic story remained, however: of a great ancient culture, embodying the primeval good religion and knowledge of humanity, which had become corrupted. It was then utterly destroyed by a catastrophic deluge, in some fashion consequent on its moral failings, leaving a few survivors to carry the memory of it, and some of its teachings, to the later world. A seventh significant feature of Druidry was that its beliefs, inevitably, put it into conflict with the professional archaeologists and historians of its time, becoming open and fierce in the 1920s and reappearing at intervals until the end of the century. This linked directly to an eighth and last feature: a general tendency for Druids to call for the reform of modern society, to make it more just, egalitarian, open-minded, and spiritualized. At times, notably in the 1910s and 1920s, this call could take on a very hard radical edge, as leading Druids denounced the rulers of their own age for intolerance, militarism, and inequality; contrasted the modern world unfavorably both with the presumed golden age of prehistory and a possible restoration of it in the future; and gave open support to institutions such as the Labour Party and events such as the General Strike.

It may be proposed, then, that these were the main characteristics of the Druidry of early and mid-twentieth-century England. How did those of the Earth Mysteries movement compare and relate to them, and what part was found for Druids in the ideas of that other movement?

Earth Mysteries in the Early Twentieth Century

The modern Earth Mysteries movement may be proposed to have arisen from two independent points, each one inspired by broader cultural developments of the time. That which is well known was represented by the work of Alfred Watkins, a Herefordshire gentleman with a comfortable private income derived from family wealth based on brewing and milling. He was a leading member of the county's historical and archaeological society, and therefore part of the traditional English social and antiquarian establishment. In 1921 he came up with the theory that prehistoric Britain had been crossed by a carefully surveyed network of straight tracks, used mainly for trade. From the beginning he linked these to a religious tradition, speculating that those who surveyed them had been a special order like Druids, and that their knowledge had been persecuted as witchcraft by medieval Christians (Watkins 1922; cf. Stout 2008: 173–7). Initially his proposals were quite well received by some fellow antiquaries, and indeed the plotting of ancient trackways and alignments was a prominent activity of people interested in British prehistory at that time (Stout 2008: 177–80; Hutton 2009: 391–2). By the end of the 1920s, however, both the old-fashioned amateur archaeologists and the newly appeared national professionals had united in rejecting them. His tracks were too straight, so that it seemed implausible that prehistoric traders would always have taken the most direct instead of the easiest route. Moreover his landscape markers for them were so diverse in nature and from so many periods that connections between them could be coincidental (Stout 2008: 182–9). Watkins turned instead to cultivating support among an uninformed general public with a love of the outdoors, who had shown an enthusiasm for his theory from the beginning. Some of them soon embodied it in a "Straight Track Club" which flourished until the Second World War, dominated by relatively affluent middle-class people who hankered after a view of very ancient culture as wiser and more "advanced" than that of historic times. In response Watkins increasingly suggested that his straight tracks, or "leys," had been laid out for religious rather than practical reasons. His followers proposed variously that the system had originated in Atlantis, or at the promptings of "Mother Earth" herself. The Druids played no part in these speculations, but their role was taken by equivalent figures such as Atlantean priests (Stout 2008: 190–214). In some ways the members of the Club represented an attempt to repossess prehistory from the new professional archaeologists, by rival members of the same social class (the bourgeoisie) and the same mind-set (ambitious and opinionated) as those professionals.

The second point of origin for the Earth Mysteries movement, it may be suggested, lay in Glastonbury, which around the beginning of the century became a center for people interested in esoteric Christianity. This was largely because of the medieval legends that associated its famous abbey with King Arthur and St Joseph of Arimathea (Hutton 2003: 62–6). One of those people was a medical doctor called John Goodchild, who yearned both for a reconciliation of the world's great historic faiths, especially Christianity and paganism, and for direct

personal communion with the God whom he believed those faiths to have worshiped in common. It may have been he, by 1904, who first discerned the apparent outline of a salmon 3,000 feet long, etched into the contours of the land between the abbey ruins and the outlying medieval chapel of Beckery to the south-west. This "Salmon of St Bride" was the very first example of what was to become one of the features of the later Earth Mysteries movement: claims to have discovered huge prehistoric figures laid out in the British landscape and hitherto unrecognized by orthodox scholars. Belief in it was certainly not confined to Goodchild himself, for in 1909 one F.C. Montagu Powell wrote to *The Spectator* to report its existence. He held that it represented the oldest and wisest of animals in the medieval Welsh story of *Culhwch ac Olwen*, and was made by the Druids to whom Glastonbury was a great holy place before Christianity came there (Benham 1993: 5–40). In this he was drawing upon two well-established ideas, both of which were by then in the process of being abandoned by leading historians. One was the belief, held by some British Christians since the sixteenth century, that Druidry had blended with Christianity to create an especially admirable Ancient British Church. The other, which had flourished since the eighteenth century, was that medieval Welsh literature contained authentic traces of Druidic belief.

Coincidentally or not, the Salmon of St Bride faded out of people's perceptions after Goodchild's death in 1914, but Druids continued to resurface in them for a while. They remained in those of Frederick Bligh Bond, the architect and archaeologist who was a leading figure in the Somerset

Archaeological Society and was engaged by the latter, and the Diocese of Bath and Wells, to excavate Glastonbury Abbey. He was removed from this position largely because of personal and institutional rivalries, but this process was made easier by his fervent belief, publicly expressed, in the validity of communications with a spirit world to support scholarly researches (Hopkinson-Ball 2007). Druids featured in some of these. In 1921, for example, a medium called Miss F. went into trance and informed Bond that Glastonbury had been a great Druidic center, dedicated to a pan-Eurasian religion of "sun and serpent," with a college of "Illuminati" to which people travelled to take higher degrees. She added that Joseph of Arimathea had not been a specific person, but an office held by Christian missionaries allied with "the Druidical orders." The stones of a prehistoric circle that had existed at Glastonbury had been built into the later abbey, to symbolize the union of the noblest aspects of both paganism and Christianity. Nonetheless, the latter was the nobler faith, sent by the Great Being himself to turn the minds of humans from too much of a preoccupation with the natural world to a higher state of being. The revelation closed with the news that the succession of spiritual leaders at Glastonbury, descended from the "Josephs," had been maintained to the present by a secret lodge of initiates (Knight 2000: 61–5). This all blended the traditional belief in a Druid-derived Ancient British Church with the trappings of late Victorian occultism.

The "Miss F." who delivered that communication was Violet Firth, who became one of the most famous of all British occultists in the twentieth century under the pen-name of Dion Fortune. In the year after she spoke this message to Bond, she was given another, addressed directly to herself by the spirit of a priest who had served in medieval Glastonbury. He restated the idea that Christianity had come easily to the area, converting the Druids from a cult of the sun to one of the "Son." The "head" center of the resulting British Church had become London, and its "heart" center Glastonbury—a very convenient formula for somebody like Fortune, who lived in the former and holidayed in the latter. The long-dead priest continued that because the Druids had handed over the forces of nature to Christianity voluntarily at Glastonbury, those forces remained unusually powerful and benevolent there. He concluded that a new age of enhanced spirituality had just opened, in which the old holy centers were reactivated. During the following weeks, Fortune received two more transmissions from the spirits of medieval churchmen, repeating the message that Glastonbury had been a place where Druid and Christian combined to produce a particularly admirable form of Christianity, which was now being reborn (Knight 2000: 72–6).

A development now occurred, however, which was to parallel that in the thinking of Watkins's followers: as the 1920s gave way to the 1930s, Druids tended to slip into the background of visions of Glastonbury as a past and present center of spiritual renewal. When Katherine Maltwood discerned a huge zodiac of stellar figures in the surrounding landscape, she credited it vaguely to the Sumerians of Mesopotamia, as the most ancient people of whom she was personally aware (Maltwood 1929). Dion Fortune herself underwent a similar shift. In the 1930s she still regarded paganism and Christianity as complementary forces, but came to identify herself much more with the former, as needed to correct the modern failings of the latter (Hutton 1999: 180–8). The paganism with which she sought to connect, however, was now one into which the Druids now fitted as latecomers, and as one prehistoric culture among others. The fount of power and wisdom to which she now looked, which had been embodied in an ancient civilization on a vast scale and was the origin of the enduring secret tradition to which she desired access, lay in Atlantis (Fortune 1934). What was happening here was that the new view of prehistory preached by mainstream scholars since the 1860s, which confined the Druids to the Iron Age, was starting to filter through to writers such as she. None the less, the faceless, nameless, prehistoric peoples who now populated earlier periods in textbooks on British archaeology, represented by their tools rather than by their spiritual works, were not acceptable substitutes for Druids to an occultist. The Atlanteans were, however, combining as they did presumed wisdom and cultural achievements of the highest kind with familiar Biblical resonances. In the portrait of them provided by Fortune, they effectively represented a blend of Druidry with ancient Egypt, the civilization which, more than any other pagan one, had exerted an influence over late-Victorian occultism.

The Rebirth of Earth Mysteries: Glastonbury

During the 1940s, both streams of the incipient Earth Mysteries movement almost ran dry: the Straight Track Club dissolved and interest in leys virtually disappeared, and a similar generation gap opened in attempts to revive Glastonbury as a modern spiritual powerhouse. Both acquired fresh energy in the 1960s, and in the case of Glastonbury this was largely imparted by Geoffrey Ashe's first book on its actual and legendary history, first published in 1957. Although confined to objective evidence, and not much interested in Maltwood's zodiac, spirit guides, or Atlantis, it was as visionary as anything produced by Goodchild, Bond, or Fortune. Its purpose was, like theirs, the spiritual and cultural renewal of the British in the modern age, using Glastonbury as the main center for this work. It was a dream to which the author had been inspired while living in Canada, before he had ever seen the place on which he focused it. His strategy was to retell all the medieval Glastonbury legends, setting them in apparent chronological order, and to argue that, since none had been conclusively disproved, they could all be believed. Mostly by back-projecting the medieval stories, he presented Glastonbury as having been a major center of pagan religion, especially under the prehistoric "Celts," which developed directly into a mysterious, exciting, and enchanting Celtic Christianity. This was by then a familiar story, and logically one in which the Druids should have played a central part, as they had earlier. Ashe, however, was determined both to exclude them and to denigrate them. He gave them four pages out of the three hundred in his book, and scorned the "supposed Secret Wisdom" which had been attributed to them. He went on to declare instead that the "concrete facts" concerning them led to a conclusion that their actual beliefs and practices had consisted of "pretentiousness and mumbo-jumbo and human sacrifice" (Ashe 1973: 24–8; cf. Hutton 2003: 66, 84).

His book provided the essential impetus for the transformation of Glastonbury into the spiritual capital of the youthful counterculture which swelled up in the Western world about ten years after it appeared. Geoffrey Ashe himself did his utmost to bring about this very result, writing in the main British magazines of the counterculture to attract its adherents. In one, *International Times*, he hailed them as the people prepared to bring about his dream for Britain (Ashe 1968). In another, *Gandalf's Garden*, he called on them to flock to Glastonbury and bring about the rebirth of its ancient power, so that it might become "a heart stirring the blood into motion again" for the British. In doing so, he warned them not to listen to professional scholars, whom he called as deranged as other members of mainstream British society, "only they are cleverer at pretending to be sane" (Ashe 1969). The same issue of that magazine contained two other articles which indicated the use that the hippie movement might make of Glastonbury and its legends. One was by Mary Caine, who resurrected Katherine Maltwood's belief in a giant zodiac inscribed on the landscape around the town, and hailed it as the greatest of all the district's antiquities and the fount of its mystique. She did not suggest who had made it, except that they had to have been people "more beautiful than they are now" who "did beautiful crazy corporate things like Stonehenge." Falling back into Biblical language, she added that "the Lord must have loved them" (Caine 1969: 17, 21). The Bible was evident again in the third contribution to that issue to concern

Glastonbury, and the only one to mention Druids. It was signed "Meiwana," and told how she had received a vision of Jesus Christ while at Glastonbury's Chalice Well. He had informed her that he had once come there himself to be initiated into the highest order of Druids, an order which had originally come out of Atlantis to create points of cosmic power in the rest of the world. Many of them, however, had turned to dark forces, which war incessantly against "the Light," but Glastonbury had remained in the hands of the good Druids. He called now on all who "turn to light" to come there to be reborn (Meiwana 1969).

There was potential here for a new lease of life for the old myth of the special aptitude of the Druids for Christianity and the special place of Britain in the early Christian world, fitted out in 1960s costume. It may be doubted, however, whether this was ever very great, because too many of those joining the counterculture were rejecting Christianity with other aspects of the parent civilization. More satisfying to these was an ancient past which pushed out the Druids and Jesus together to focus on the Atlanteans, who carried much less baggage from established beliefs. Four months after this burst of articles came one in a mainstream newspaper, the *Guardian*, which hailed the Glastonbury landscape as impregnated with the "cosmic power" of "Atlantean days," manifested most clearly in the zodiac (Anon. 1969). Thereafter Druids made little appearance in the publications of the counterculture that made Glastonbury its home during the following decade. One of the few to give them any place was a Londoner who had settled there after his attention had first been drawn to the place by Ashe: Anthony Roberts. He was unusual both in his willingness to embrace the idea of a prehistory divided into successive phases like that of the mainstream archaeologists and his lack of interest in nonhistorical civilizations such as Atlantis. This was despite the fact that most of the features which he regarded as prehistoric monuments were not accepted as such by most of the archaeologists. In his scheme, the first constructed there was Maltwood's zodiac, laid out by unknown people at any time between 10,000 and 2700 BCE. Then came astronomer priests, around 2000 BCE, who put up standing stones and developed the Chalice Well as a holy place. Next were the Druids, who built a huge spiral labyrinth around the dominant hill of the district, Glastonbury Tor, as one nodal point for Alfred Watkins's ley system. Finally Christianity arrived, and here Roberts held to the old idea that it had first embraced aspects of the preceding paganism, but then denied and obliterated them as it grew more powerful and worldly in the course of the Middle Ages (Roberts 1977). His thinking, like that of earlier twentieth-century authors on the spirituality of the town and its district, embodied a substantial residue of Christianity. He wrote that prehistoric sites and the natural forces that they embodied were "the crystallisation of the Divine patterns projected on to Creation by the all-encompassing Will of God" (Roberts 1984: 3).

The Rebirth of Earth Mysteries: Leys

A renaissance of interest in Watkins's leys occurred in the 1960s as a spin-off from one of the most dynamic areas of unorthodox scientific enquiry in the 1950s: an interest in

Unidentified Flying Objects. In 1961 a young man called Tony Wedd published the idea that leys might have been markers for flight paths for alien spacecraft, which had been visiting our planet for many millennia. Once again there was a strong religious current to his thought, as he declared that the extra-terrestrials had multiplied their visits in the mid-twentieth century to prepare humans for "A Golden Age of Peace and Justice," much like gods or angels; indeed, he subsequently termed them simply "gods." He converted to his enthusiasm a Surrey schoolboy, Philip Heselton, who founded a Ley-Hunter's Club and the *Ley Hunter* magazine to propagate it; he in turn fired up a fellow pupil, Jimmy Goddard, who lectured on the subject for the next few years, and in doing so attracted the attention of a Londoner, John Michell (Wedd 1972).

It was Michell who brought these ideas to a much wider public. His first book on them, *Flying Saucer Vision*, in 1967, restated Wedd's views at much greater length, holding that the development of the human race had been influenced by "gods" from the sky, who had rejected it when it turned too greedily to material and technological goals. That materialist obsession was now bringing it close to self-destruction, which could be averted by renewing contact with the gods, and in the process reactivating the ancient holy centers which had promoted such contact (Michell 1967a). Two years later he published the book which, more than any other, defined and energized the revived ley-hunting movement, *The View Over Atlantis*. He combined Watkins's leys with the Chinese mythology of *lung mei*, lines of energy which ran across the surface of the earth and with which humans needed to live in harmony to prosper, especially when placing buildings. In Michell's portrait, the leys had been laid out to harness this energy, magnetic in form and rising naturally from the earth. They had been the work of a scientific and religious elite which had visited almost every corner of the globe and planted a network of megalithic structures upon it to channel the earth energy for the good of humanity (Michell 1969). Once again, the book embodied a fervent post-Christian religiosity. It had the Biblical belief in a former universal, good, and true system of belief and knowledge, which had decayed because of the unworthiness of later generations. Its tone was evangelical and apocalyptic, announcing the dawning of the Age of Aquarius, in which tyrants would fall, the power of "old magicians" be destroyed, and the ancient wisdom be restored. It predicted that, as part of that restoration, humanity would regain "the former belief in revelation on which the science of the ancient world was founded." To Michell, that science had been objectively correct, and the energy currents on which it had been based were really there. He made clear that the rediscovery of this ancient wisdom involved more than an exercise in scholarship: it was a reconnection to divinity. He concluded the book with the proclamation that such a reconnection represented "the rediscovery of access to the divine will" and "the restoration of the Holy Spirit" (Michell 1969: vii, 185). Combined with this evangelical rhetoric was the spirit of 1960s "Big Science," for to Michell the worldwide ley system had been not merely a partnership with divinity but a "great scientific instrument." The men who had laid it out had represented a "common scientific

programme and network" transcending races and nationalities (Michell 1969: 62–4).

Among the "magicians" whom he hoped to see thrown from power were modern archaeologists, whom he accused of mere "treasure hunting and grave robbery" (Michell 1969: 64). His definition of the wrong sort of archaeologist was absolutely consistent: it comprised everybody who had accepted and implemented the Victorian revolution in attitudes to prehistory which had introduced the Darwinian theory of evolution and the division of the ancient past into ages based on technological advancement. He expressed considerable admiration for scholars from earlier periods, such as John Aubrey, who had first suggested that megalithic monuments had been built by Druids; William Stukeley, who had made it orthodoxy; and the Welsh literary expert Iolo Morganwg, who had published a system of theology and ritual which he represented as that of the Druids but had in fact devised himself (Hutton 2009: 65–73, 86–124, 146–82). He also celebrated, and was influenced by, others who had come later and challenged the new archaeological orthodoxy in the name of a universal or pan-Eurasian system of ancient wisdom, notably the astronomer Sir Norman Lockyer, Alfred Watkins, and Frederick Bligh Bond. He also accepted the work of a respected contemporary academic, a Professor of Engineering, Alexander Thom, who argued that megalithic monuments had been laid out with considerable mathematical and astronomical learning and according to a common plan. In part this pattern simply reflected a general hostility to current orthodoxy, so that anybody who was pitted against it could be made into a hero. It also, however, consisted of a rebellion against the secularism of the new archaeology: Michell was turning, instinctively, to traditions which invested ancient monuments with a sense of spirituality and of connection to divine teachings. In a letter to a magazine of the counterculture, in 1967, he had declared, in Old Testament style, that only the "wilfully blind" could be unaware of the signs of "an imminent revelation" that was to be made to the human race (Michell 1967b: 15).

His attack on excavation, as the main professional tool of archaeologists, had an additional context. This was the very period in which those professionals had both decreed the unearthing and interpretation of artifacts to be the definitive activity of their discipline and achieved an absolute monopoly of it. Faced with this monopoly, it is not surprising that many young (or youngish) people who felt an interest in ancient monuments chose not to engage in the persistence and hard labor needed to gain admission to it. Instead they followed the older tradition of the passionate and independent amateur, in the few remaining pursuits now open to one: the tracing of apparent trackways or power lines; dowsing; the detection of possible alignments of ancient monuments on heavenly bodies; and the making of a sensuous personal relationship with prehistoric sites. Ironically, all these were themselves rooted in practices and writings which had been around longer than professional archaeology and helped to give birth to the latter (Hutton 2009: 387–93). There was also, perhaps, a social dimension to the opposition. The proponents of the new countercultural prehistory consisted in some respects of an alliance of groups opposed to the

upwardly mobile bourgeois meritocrats who embodied the new professionalized archaeology. John Michell himself had been given the classic upbringing of a member of the traditional elite, at Eton College and Cambridge University, and had inherited a private fortune (Lachman 2001: 371–2; Schreiber and Nicholson 1987). There was more than a touch of aristocratic hauteur in his treatment of middle-class professionals. Phil Russell, alias Wally Hope, the moving spirit behind the foundation of the Stonehenge festival which became the prime expression of the 1970s and 1980s mystical counterculture, had likewise inherited substantial private means, which relieved him of the need to work for a living (Stone 1996: 79–99). In a coalition of shared interests with them were individuals such as Paul Screeton, who refounded the *Ley Hunter* magazine at the end of 1969 and was rooted in northern working-class culture, and grammar-schoolboys like Philip Heselton and Jimmy Goddard, who wanted to make their mark on an understanding of the ancient past without submitting to the qualifying process now demanded by academic power brokers.

The View Over Atlantis provoked a rush of other books and of magazine articles, continuing through the 1970s and 1980s, and a new upsurge in ley-hunting. Two books from the mid-1970s may be regarded as especially important landmark works in the maturation of the Earth Mysteries movement. One was Screeton's *Quicksilver Heritage*, in 1974, which developed Michell's view of prehistory to suggest that the Neolithic had been an era in which humanity devoted itself wholly to spirituality, and that the fall from grace occurred with the invention of metalworking. He suggested, likewise, that the golden age of prehistory might now be restored, as "a new breed of Britons look to the countryside for a true vision of the past and find themselves also exploring the infinity of the mind's inner space" (Screeton 1974: 13, 67–73). Like Michell, he was convinced that the energy flowing along the leys was an objectively real, and perennial, force (Screeton 1984: 5). The other work was *Mysterious Britain* by Janet and Colin Bord, in 1972, which embedded the ideas of authors such as Michell and contributors to *The Ley Hunter* in a gazetteer of ancient sites, combining undoubted prehistoric monuments with controversial examples such as the Glastonbury Zodiac as common relics of a single ancient culture (Bord and Bord 1972). The emphasis in this book was on the mystery presented by these relics, as the title suggests, rather than on an evangelism made possible by a confident interpretation of them. Nonetheless, Colin Bord at least had been inspired by a religiosity as great as that of other personalities in the movement. Three years earlier he had published his belief in a sophisticated civilization which had existed on a land mass in the Pacific called Mu, and had colonized most other parts of the globe, before its parent continent was drowned in a natural cataclysm 12,000 years ago. In particular, it taught "the pure simple religion that at later ages was corrupted and perverted," and with it the message that the destruction of the continent was itself the fault of its inhabitants, in falling out of harmony with the planet. This myth was in fact the British answer to the American Atlantis, developed at the end of the nineteenth century, and behind both Mu and

Atlantis lay the Book of Genesis. Bord, of course, warned his readers that the modern world was facing destruction for the same reasons as the people of Mu, unless they repented and accepted once more their place as "an integral part of the Creator's concept, with a definite purpose which he will eventually fulfil" (Bord 1969: 4–8).

Earth Mysteries and Modern Druids

By the 1970s, the newly revived Earth Mysteries movement and modern Druidry coexisted as prominent manifestations of "alternative" spirituality, with a constant and significant impact on public awareness. An obvious question that arises is how the adherents of each regarded the other; and it reveals a consistent and significant pattern. One Druid chief certainly reached out to Earth Mysteries with great enthusiasm: Ross Nichols, leader of the newly established Order of Bards, Ovates, and Druids which had seceded from the Universal Bond in 1964. This was part of a love affair which Nichols conducted with the new counterculture as a whole. He incorporated the new set of alleged Glastonbury monuments, such as the zodiac and the spiral labyrinth, into his view of ancient Druidry, and his order held ceremonies on Glastonbury Tor rather than at the more traditional Stonehenge (Nichols 1990: 17, 207–16). He adopted the ideas of John Michell, contributed to the *Ley Hunter* and wrote to the *International Times* to suggest that the "hippie" counterculture had a natural alliance with Druids (Nichols 1970; 1971; and 1990: 188–97, 262–4). To some extent, those within that counterculture reciprocated by viewing Druids, in turn, as "hip" figures equally at war with the "establishment." A guide to "alternative London" published in 1971 included the Universal Bond among a list of spiritual groups recommended to readers. The following year Pan American Airlines offered a "Psychic Tour" of Britain, including "a day at Stonehenge with the Chief Druid," presumably the leader of the Universal Bond (Loach 1973: 97, 107).

These interchanges were, however, essentially peripheral. The elderly men and women who led the Universal Bond remained more or less aloof from the youthful enthusiasm of Earth Mysteries researchers and the culture of hippiedom in which most of the latter were embedded. For their part, the attitude to Druidry of those researchers was, like that of their harbinger Geoffrey Ashe, at best condescending and at worst chilly. Admirers of the Druids in the eighteenth and nineteenth centuries had characterized the ancient Britain over which they had presided as a place of megalithic monuments, great wisdom based on close observation of the natural world, harmony with that world, social peace, and personal freedom. This view was now applied to the Neolithic by John Michell and his allies, but with Druids removed from the picture. Instead, they were relegated to the very end of prehistory: virtually the only major tenet of the secularized archaeology which had appeared under Victoria that Earth Mysteries researchers did adopt. Michell himself termed Druids latecomers who had never fully understood the great old knowledge of the ley system that they had inherited. In his view, the early Christian Churches had actually comprehended it better, and the

Druids had yielded to them easily because they recognized Christianity as "a more glorious expression of their own tradition, now degenerate" (Michell 1969: 25, 31–4, 161–84). Likewise, Paul Screeton dismissed the Druids as "elitist and corrupted." He added that they had inherited the ley system from the truly wise people of the Neolithic, "but my guess is that they understood it less well than we do." He recognized that at least one modern Druid, Ross Nichols, spoke the same language as ley-hunters, but with the caution that Nichols had learned from people like Screeton, rather than vice versa (Screeton 1974: 195–7). The most significant reference to Druids in the Bords's guide to British monuments came when readers were told that they probably had nothing to do with Stonehenge (Bord and Bord 1972: 4). The most generous reference to them made by a prominent member of the 1970s Earth Mysteries network (and later one of the leading figures in reshaping its ideas) came in an early article by Nigel Pennick. He suggested that the ancient Druids "were capable of acts that today would be classed miraculous or impossible," adding that this was "an established historic fact." Nonetheless, he still emphasized that they came along long after the time of megalithic monuments, and that the people of that earlier time had been capable of even greater knowledge and achievement (Pennick 1970).

Druids, ancient or modern, did no better out of another great tradition to emerge as an alternative to orthodox prehistory in the late twentieth century: the "Goddess Movement" which commenced in the late 1970s and peaked in the 1980s and early 1990s. Whereas ley-hunting was in origin quintessentially English, this movement was an American phenomenon, though with a significant impact on Europe (Morgan 1996; Harvey 1997: 69–86, 143–5; Hutton 1999: 340–68). In England its ideology combined at times with aspects of that held by many Earth Mysteries researchers (Sjöö and Mor 1987; Lonegren 1991; Straffon 1997), especially in a common belief in numinous powers that existed naturally within the surface of the planet. To many devotees of the Goddess, indeed, the planet was itself the living body of their deity. Another link with Earth Mysteries was the manner in which this movement reasserted some ideas derived ultimately from the Bible; indeed, it did so with still greater clarity. It depended on a belief in the practice in earliest human times of a benevolent and essentially correct religion dedicated to a single divinity, which covered the whole of the European and Mediterranean worlds but had an epicenter in the Near East. This Biblical model was adapted by it in three ways. First, the lost golden age was identified specifically with the Palaeolithic and Neolithic, which now occupied the symbolic space of the Book of Genesis. Second, and especially in the writings of the single leading archaeologist to become a convert, Marija Gimbutas, the epicenter was in Turkey and the Balkans, rather than in Palestine (Gimbutas 1989 and 1991). Third and most important, it had a female deity and a female-centered society. As in the earlier belief system, this good religion and society, in harmony with fellow humanity, the natural world, and the divine, was corrupted into the polytheistic paganism and the warlike and unequal societies that existed by the time that history dawned. In this case, however, a different mechanism

was proposed to explain the corruption, instead of the inherent degeneracy of fallen human nature, as represented in the Bible. This was the inherent degeneracy of male human nature. In some earlier formulations of Goddess movement literature, this was assumed to have welled up internally and destroyed the golden age from within. Marija Gimbutas, however, linked it to the late-Victorian identification of invasions by new races as the motor force of prehistory, which dominated academic thought for most of the twentieth century. In particular she adopted a specific component of that model, the belief in an eruption of new peoples from the east into the European Neolithic. In this interpretation, the newcomers had introduced a bad religion and a bad social system, both dominated by men and therefore naturally more violent, repressive, exploitative, and unequal.

The modern religion of the Goddess could dispose of a condemnatory and apocalyptic rhetoric as fierce as that of any Christian. Not only did it regard historic, male-dominated cultures as inherently evil and deserving of complete reformation (or demolition) but, in view of the growing and very real fears of global ecological catastrophe consequent on modern industrial living, it could argue that failure to adopt its belief system inevitably doomed the world to destruction. In all these respects, it drew directly on the American evangelical tradition in which it was rooted; though it may be noted that the British Earth Mysteries movement had been itself just as capable of holding out a choice of salvation or destruction to humanity, consequent upon whether its message was or was not generally adopted. The matriarchal view of prehistory had even less time for Druids than ley-hunters, as the former appeared all too clearly to be a male priesthood produced by the cultures that had destroyed the Neolithic golden age.

Druidry and Earth Mysteries: A Twentieth-century Relationship

Near the opening of this article, eight characteristics were suggested as definitive for modern English Druidry. It remains now to see how the Earth Mysteries movement matches up against these. The first, of being distinctively twentieth-century, certainly makes a fit. Although Earth Mysteries, like spiritual Druidry, drew on older ideas, the distinctive features of both first appeared in the first three decades of the century. The Druids developed faster, in that their movement was already coherent and well known by the 1920s, whereas the full flowering of Earth Mysteries only occurred in the 1970s, but the component ideas of the latter were almost fully formed by 1930. The second characteristic—that the modern Druids treated prehistoric sites, and especially megaliths, as living sacred places— was also a core feature of Earth Mysteries. Both, moreover, tended to view prehistory as a continuum of belief and practice, and indeed one of the central properties of leys was that they connected ceremonial sites from all millennia until and including the Christian Middle Ages. Both drew upon older scholarly orthodoxy, and indeed on much the same antiquarian heroes: of those praised by John Michell, William Stukeley was claimed as a former chief by the Universal Bond, and Iolo Morganwg's writings supplied the main rituals employed by that Druid order from the 1950s onward. Both, though

often unconsciously, clung in many ways to views of the remote past based on the Bible, and especially to a belief in an original, universal, good, and natural religion, which had subsequently become corrupted and almost forgotten to the great detriment of humanity. Both in turn held out hope that our species might, by changing its ideas and practices, return to its primeval state of bliss. Both made comparatively slight, but still significant, use of the modernized myth of Atlantis, and came into intermittent but fierce conflict with professional archaeologists and historians. As one aspect of this conflict, both called for the reform and renewal of modern society, to make it more just, spiritualized, and harmonious, both when dealing with its own members and in its treatment of the planet.

The complete identity of the two movements, throughout this checklist, makes them seem more like dual expressions of a single twentieth-century English spirituality, drawing on a common reverence for and sense of kinship with the natural or rural worlds and the prehistoric peoples who had lived upon and with those worlds. This raises still more vividly the questions of why relations between the two groups, during their time of full coexistence in the 1960s and 1970s, should have been so limited, and why leading Earth Mysteries researchers, in particular, were either condescending, dismissive, or hostile toward Druidry. As none of the protagonists themselves has considered the matter, explanations must be inferred, and there is perhaps an obvious one to make: that some of the worst tensions have always existed within families, and different groups within movements— whether the latter be religious, spiritual, political, cultural, or social—are characterized by mutual rivalry and competition at least as often as by cooperation. In this case, however, a more precise reason may be proposed. By the time that Geoffrey Ashe wrote in the 1950s, let alone when John Michell and his companions did in the following two decades, Druids of the Universal Bond variety had long been established as familiar personalities in the public eye. In one sense they still represented a radical, challenging, and avant-garde spirituality. In another, with their by then long genuine history extending back to the limits of living memory, and their much longer legendary history, fully developed by the 1950s and taking the order back to 1717 (Hutton 2009: 379–82), they looked more like establishment figures themselves. Such a role was emphasized by their annual rites at Stonehenge, when they took center stage at the monument while the general public was increasingly excluded from it at that time in order to make space for them (Hutton 2009: 385–7, 396–9). It does seem that attitudes to them among Earth Mysteries writers reproduced those, in my own experience, of people attending the (self-called) People's Free Festival at Stonehenge in the period 1974–84, with whom, indeed, those writers overlapped. These were sometimes appreciative and supportive, but often mocking and resentful, viewing the Druids as a quasi-priesthood who seemed aloof from the festival itself and automatically took over the stones, and assumed a privileged position there, when they appeared. The literature of the Universal Bond, moreover, claimed an esoteric knowledge of ancient Britain, superior to that of nonmembers, which made no mention of, and seemed to have no obvious place for, phenomena such as Unidentified Flying Objects and leys. It is

hard to resist the suspicion that a resentment of the privileges and pretensions of the modern Druids lay behind much of the tendency of Earth Mysteries writers to deny ancient Druids, and therefore their modern counterparts, any great importance.

A final common feature of Druidry and Earth Mysteries was that the form of both, and the relationship between them, began to change dramatically in the later 1980s. In 1985 the Universal Bond was banned from holding its customary public ceremonies at Stonehenge, as part of the operation that suppressed the Free Festival, and faded into relative obscurity. Its place in the public eye was taken by a large number of new Druid orders founded or refounded in the following ten years. All very firmly ascribed to the name and the identity of modern Druids, but they tended to be much less influenced by Christianity than the older orders, and much more inclined (however selectively) to take on ideas from Earth Mysteries: indeed, a newly recreated Order of Bards, Ovates, and Druids made John Michell its Presider. Some of the other new Druid groups combined overtly pagan religion with hands-on radical politics (Hutton 2003: 239–58; and 2007: 194–204). In many ways, the new Druidry came to represent the main spiritual face of British counterculture, not least because it had absorbed many of the ideas of the Earth Mysteries and Goddess movements. Over the same period, the initial energy of the Goddess Movement itself began to run down, while followers of Earth Mysteries split into mutually hostile factions, a process complete by the end of the century. Earth Mysteries researchers who prospered most, and made the greatest impact on wider society, were those who came to cooperate with a professional archaeology which was now starting enthusiastically to embrace preoccupations—such as an engagement with landscape and with the cognitive properties of sites—which had been aspects of the Earth Mysteries (Trubshaw 2005: 59–108; Stout 2006: 18–34). By contrast, those who continued to emphasize the religious and mystical qualities of the movement and employed an apocalyptic language—so prominent in the years around 1970—have fallen almost completely into the background. Those modern counterparts of Noah's Flood—Atlantis and Mu—seem now likewise to be disappearing from modern "alternative" spirituality.

A comparison of modern Druidry and Earth Mysteries has therefore another value for the historian: to illumine a cultural shift of tremendous importance in modern British society, namely the abandonment of the Bible as the ultimate foundation on which views of the prehistoric human past are built. At first sight it may seem as if establishment scholars did this in the mid-Victorian period, when they took Darwin and the three-age system as their model instead of Genesis. At a more insidious level, however, the Biblical images persisted even in orthodox prehistory, as until the mid-twentieth century leading archaeologists continued to visualize the remote past in terms of a single original religion serving a single great deity; of the diffusion of civilization from a single point of origin (usually in the Near East); and of waves of invading and conquering peoples (always crossing over from the east) settling new territories as their promised lands (Hutton 2009: 310–12). These only decisively disappeared in the 1980s and 1990s, with

the emergence of a "post-processual" archaeology, which saw prehistory in terms of dispersed and local religious traditions rather than unifying faiths, and of a consumer choice between cultural packages, instead of grand structures of belief. "Peer-polity interaction" has replaced racial groupings and invasions as the motor force of cultural change. In this, intellectual attitudes are undoubtedly reflecting the changed nature of Western society by the end of the twentieth century. The flourishing forms of modern Paganism that have spread through that society since the 1950s, and especially since the 1970s, have likewise looked to diversity as the keynote of contemporary spirituality. The themes of a single true original religion, based on divine revelation; of the natural corruptibility of humanity and its tendency to pervert and misunderstand divine teachings; and of the need to reform religious belief and reclaim old truths to avoid wholesale destruction, all seem to be vanishing from counter-cultural tradition just as from orthodox scholarship.

This has come about, it may be suggested, not just because of the development of a secularized, pick-and-mix society but because of the loss of a traditional education. The generation which came of age in England in the 1950s and 1960s was probably the last to be schooled automatically in Bible stories. This process made it easy for it, as for those before, to understand many of the reference points of traditional European art and literature, which are opaque to anybody without that grounding. Those that have come after do not possess this advantage; but they may have made an equivalent gain in the process. It seems to have been in the 1970s, and not the 1860s, that English society, at least, began finally to break loose from the Bible when contemplating the remote past. In doing so, it may have achieved a novel conceptual freedom, which might make a loss of direct contact with past cultures worthwhile. This, it may be proposed, is the last and greatest perception to be furnished to a historian by a comparison of twentieth-century English Druidry with the Earth Mysteries movement.

References

Anon., 1969. "The Hippie Vale of Avalon." *Guardian*, 20 December: 8.

Ashe, G., 1968. "Letter from an Over 30." *International Times* 38: 15.

Ashe, G., 1969. "Glastonbury, Key to the Future." *Gandalf's Garden* 4: 15.

Ashe, G., 1973 [1957].[setter, stet these sq bracs: part of text, not tag] *King Arthur's Avalon*. London: Fontana reprint.

Benham, P., 1993. *The Avalonians*. Glastonbury: Gothic Image.

Bord, C., 1969. "The Cosmic Continent." *Gandalf's Garden* 6: 4–8.

Bord, J. and Bord, C., 1972. *Mysterious Britain*. London: Garnstone.

Caine, M., 1969. "The Glastonbury Giants." *Gandalf's Garden* 4: 16–21.

Devereux, P., 1994. *The New Ley-Hunter's Guide*. Glastonbury: Gothic Image.

Fortune, D., 1934. *Avalon of the Heart*. London: Aquarian.

Gimbutas, M., 1989. *The Language of the Goddess*. London: Thames & Hudson.

Gimbutas, M., 1991. *The Civilisation of the Goddess*. San Francisco: Harper and Row.

Harvey, G., 1997. *Listening People, Speaking Earth*. London: Hurst.

Hopkinson-Ball, T., 2007. *The Rediscovery of Glastonbury: Frederick Bligh Bond, Architect of the New Age*. Stroud: Sutton.

Hutton, R., 1999. *The Triumph of the Moon: A History of Modern Pagan Witchcraft*. Oxford: Oxford University Press.

Hutton, R., 2003. *Witches, Druids and King Arthur: Studies in Paganism, Myth and Magic*. London: Hambledon and London.

Hutton, R., 2007. *The Druids*. London: Hambledon Continuum.

Hutton, R, 2009. *Blood and Mistletoe: The History of the Druids in Britain*. London: Yale University Press.

Knight, G., 2000. *Dion Fortune and the Inner Light*. Loughborough: Thoth.

Lachman, G.V., 2001. *Turn Off Your Mind: The Mystic Sixties and the Dark Side of the Age of Aquarius*. London: Sidgwick & Jackson.

Loach, K., 1973. *Youthquake*. London: Sheldon.

Lonegren, S., 1991. *Labyrinths: Ancient Myths and Modern Uses*. Glastonbury: Gothic Image.

Maltwood, K., 1929. *A Guide to Glastonbury's Temple of the Stars*. London: Clarke.

Meiwana, 1969. "Jesus and the Druids." *Gandalf's Garden* 4: 14–15.

Michell, J., 1967a. *The Flying Saucer Vision: The Holy Grail Restored*. London: Sidgwick & Jackson.

Michell, J., 1967b. "Letter." *The Image*, 71.

Michell, J., 1969. *The View Over Atlantis*. London: Sago.

Morgan, L., 1996. "Women and the Goddess Today", in G. Harvey and C. Hardman (eds), *Paganism Today*. London: Thorsons, pp. 94–108.

Nichols, R., 1970. "Advertisement." *The Ley Hunter* 14: n.p.

Nichols, R., 1971. "Letter." *International Times* 115: 15.

Nichols, R., 1990. *The Book of Druidry*. London: Aquarian.

Pennick, N., 1970. "Geomancy." *The Ley Hunter* 13: 11–12.

Pennick, N. and Devereux, P., 1989. *Lines on the Landscape*. London: Hale.

Roberts, A., 1977. "Glastonbury, The Ancient Avalon", in A. Roberts (ed.), *Glastonbury: Ancient Avalon, New Jerusalem*. Tiptree: Rider, pp. 10–25.

Roberts, A., 1984. "Contract Killers (Psychic Cripples)." *The Shaman* 4: 3–4.

Schreiber, L. and Nicholson, J., 1987. *An English Figure*. London: Bozo.

Screeton, P., 1974. *Quicksilver Heritage*. Wellingborough: Thorsons.

Screeton, P., 1984. "Ley-Line Detractors in Question." *The Shaman* 4: 5–7.

Screeton, P., 1984–5. "Seekers of the Linear Vision." serialized in *Stonehenge Viewpoint* nos. 44–51.

Sjöö, M., and Mor, B., 1987. *The Great Cosmic Mother*. San Francisco: Harper and Row.

Stone, C.J., 1996. *Fierce Dancing: Adventures in the Underground*. London: Faber & Faber.

Stout, A., 2005. *Universal Majesty, Verity and Love Infinite: A Life of George Watson MacGregor Reid*. Lewes: Order of Bards, Ovates and Druids. Available at http://druidry.org/pdfs/fifth mt haemus lecture.pdf.

Stout, A., 2006. *What's Real and What's Not: Reflections upon Archaeology and Earth Mysteries in Britain*. Frome: Runetree.

Stout, A, 2008. *Creating Prehistory: Druids, Ley Hunters and Archaeologists in Pre-War Britain*. Oxford: Blackwell.

Straffon, C., 1997. *The Earth Goddess*. London: Blandford.

Trubshaw, B., 2005. *Sacred Places: Prehistory and Popular Imagination*. Wymeswold: Heart of Albion.

Watkins, A., 1922. *Early British Trackways*. Hereford: Watkins Motor Company.

Wedd, J.A.D., 1972. *Skyways and Landmarks*. Hull: Star Fellowship.

Time and Mind:
The Journal of
Archaeology,
Consciousness
and Culture

Volume 2—Issue 3
November 2009
pp. 333–346

DOI:
10.2752/175169609X12464529903218

The Logic of Empirical Proof
A Note on the Course of the Beckhampton Avenue

Lionel Sims

Lionel Sims is head of anthropology at the University of East
London, Vice President of the Society of Cultural Astronomy
in Europe (SEAC), and a member of the Stonehenge
Round Table hosted by English Heritage. His research into
ancient monuments was the subject of the "Stonehenge
Rediscovered" commissioned by National Geographic.
L.D.Sims@uel.ac.uk

Abstract

After 150 years of archaeological skepticism toward Stukeley's
nineteenth-century claim for a Beckhampton avenue in
the Avebury monuments, Gillings et al. (2008) have finally
confirmed that it did in fact exist. However, *contra* Stukeley,
they only allow its existence up to the site of the "Longstones
Cove," and dispute its continuation further to the south-
west to Fox Covert, as claimed by Stukeley. This article
attempts to demonstrate that by documentary method, field
survey, geophysics, site excavation, and the method of critical
experiment, this interpretation fails the normal standards
of the logic of empirical proof. This failure to sustain their
case leaves Stukeley's claim for the Beckhampton avenue
continuing to Fox Covert standing and open to further
investigation.

Keywords: Stukeley; Beckhampton avenue; Avebury;
proof, archaeoastronomy

The Beckhampton Avenue is one of two avenues of parallel
rows of stones claimed by William Stukeley to be part of
the Avebury monument complex in Wiltshire, England. The
Avebury complex includes the largest prehistoric stone circle
and earth mound in the world: Silbury Hill (Burl 2002). The
antiquarian Stukeley's 1743 view of the complex in Fig 1

shows the Beckhampton Avenue "starting" at Fox Covert and approaching the Avebury circle from the south-west across the River Winterbourne. The avenue is roughly symmetrical to another avenue, the West Kennet Avenue, which exits the Avebury circle to the south-east and follows the course of a dry valley to "terminate" at a smaller stone and post circle named "The Sanctuary." The Avebury monuments were built in the third millennium BC and are about 20 miles north of Stonehenge.[1]

Until 1999, many British archaeologists doubted Stukeley's claim for the existence of the Beckhampton Avenue, including Lukis, Piggot, Ucko, Pollard, Gillings, Whittle, Thomas, and Parker-Pearson (for whom see discussion and references in Gillings and Pollard 2004: 6 and Gillings et al. 2008: 58–62). Their view before 1999 was that very few stones could be observed along the claimed route, and that therefore Stukeley's testimony could not be trusted. This doubt was set by some archaeologists in the latter half of the nineteenth century, when it was considered improbable that an avenue would cross a river, and that the very few stones to the west of the geophysics survey could be more parsimoniously explained as remnants of other unconnected features.

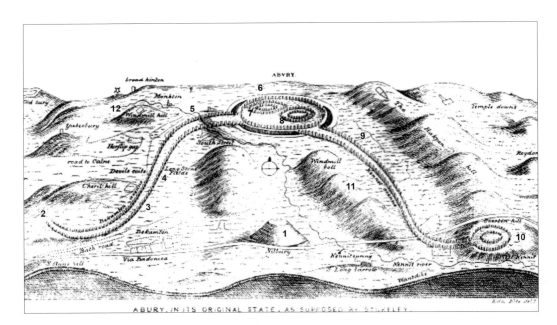

Fig 1 Stukeley's "A Scenographic view of the Druid temple at Avebury in north Wiltshire as in its original"
Key: 1 Silbury Hill; 2 Fox Covert; 3 Beckhampton Avenue; 4 Adam's Cove/Longstones Enclosure; 5 River Winterbourne; 6 Avebury Circle; 7 northern inner circle; 8 southern inner circle; 9 West Kennet Avenue; 10 Sanctuary; 11 Waden Hill; 12 Windmill Hill (adapted from Mortimer 2003: 50–1)

However, there has always been another constituency within British archaeology that accepted the existence of the Beckhampton Avenue. While initially skeptical, when the western entrance to the Avebury circle was rediscovered by Alexander Keiller in 1939, he changed his view and accepted the possibility of a Beckhampton Avenue. Keiller together with King, Twining, Stukeley, Smith, Burl, and Vatcher all support the view that the Beckhampton Avenue existed and continued to Fox Covert. The issue was always therefore one of *interpretation* on the basis of incomplete evidence, and the professional disinclination of many archaeologists to accept Stukeley derives from a long-held and arguably overly-skeptical and ambiguous frame of mind toward his work (Ucko et al. 1991: 240).

Since 1999, fieldwork conducted by Gillings et al. has led them, like Keiller before, to change their mind on the existence of the Beckhampton Avenue (Gillings et al. 2008). Geophysical surveys and digs carried out between 1999 and 2003 found paired rows of buried stones and stone holes to the east of Adam's Cove (Fig 2) "exactly where he [Stukeley] had identified it" (Gillings and Pollard 2004: 19). This rediscovered avenue overlay an earlier structure—the Longstones Enclosure. Gillings et al. and Pollard now argue that in fact the Beckhampton Avenue did exist and ran a course from the Avebury Circle to the Longstone Cove but, contra Stukeley, they argue it did *not* extend further to the south-west to terminate at Fox Covert. The main evidence for this claim is that a geophysics survey and 50m x 40m

Fig 2 The Longstones, "Adam" and "Eve" (photo: Paul Devereux)

trench dug immediately to the south-west of the "Adam" stone failed to reveal any buried stones or stone-holes (Gillings et al. 2008: 71). As they invoke the criteria of empirical proof, then this claim can itself be subjected to the accepted standards of inference and proof.

Evidence from Antiquarian Testimony

Two destruction episodes, one in the late Middle Ages and another in the early eighteenth century, denuded much of the Avebury monuments. Reputable antiquarian testimony is important for us today since it was made before some of the destruction had been completed. But Stukeley's was not the only or the first antiquarian report of the Beckhampton Avenue. Independent of and before Stukeley, Reverend Twining also reported that the Beckhampton Avenue continued on to Fox Covert (Burl 2002: 218; Gillings et al. 2008: 365–6; Peterson 2003).

Two identical but independent testimonies suggest that they were both drawing upon local folk knowledge of the monuments. In fact "… several decades later, the curate of Avebury, Reverend Lucas recorded that an elderly parishioner, John Clements, could still point out the line of the avenue at the time of his death." (Malone 1989: 93) and "Stukeley was reliant on oral history for much of his information" (Ucko et al. 1991: 182). Since two antiquarians and a folk culture independently came up with similar claims, this raises the credibility of any one of them.

The archaeological reticence to accept Stukeley's testimony for a Fox Covert start/terminus location for the Beckhampton Avenue (Fig 3) is partly based upon the suspicion that he made its course fit his post-1725 "serpent" theory of the monuments, in which the Beckhampton Avenue, Avebury, West Kennet Avenue, Sanctuary, and other monuments formed the shape of a snake

Fig 3 A view near the spot of the termination of the Beckhampton Avenue, according to Stukeley, July 19, 1723 (Mortimer 2003: 68)

in the landscape, and that this degrades the validity of his documentary evidence. This raises a number of issues that were resolved by Ucko nearly two decades ago (Ucko et al. 1991). First, the claim for a Fox Covert "start" to the avenue was made before 1725. Second, the presumption within archaeology that Stukeley's pre-1725 field data is accurate compared to his post-1725 "serpent" record is not justified (Ucko 1991: 244). Third, before 1725 he developed a geomantic theory by which the avenues and circle followed a rigorous symmetry around Silbury Hill, and he predicted the Fox Covert "start" would have a temple just as the West Kennet "terminus" had the Sanctuary. After intensive fieldwork failed to locate such a temple he dropped this claim, and started searching for other interpretive hypotheses for the Beckhampton Avenue (Ucko et al. 1991: 87). In short, the integrity of the field data took precedence over the theory. Fourth, it is inconsistent for Gillings et al. to reject Stukeley as a valid documentary source with respect to the Fox Covert claim, but to accept it as a fieldwork and excavation site guide for other research strategies, e.g. where to locate their exploratory trenches around the Trusloe Cottages (Gillings et al. 2008: 105); accepting Stukeley's accuracy for the location of the West Kennet Cove as under the road for not testing for its existence (Gillings and Pollard 2004: 20); the Beckhampton Avenue's course around West Kennet village (Gillings et al. 2008, 129–33). Fifth, there is a qualitative difference between the detailed descriptive sections of Stukeley's record compared to the interpretive sections. For example, in the Stukeley "Stonehenge 1723" manuscript held at Cardiff Central Reference Library

there is a loose sheet recording Stukeley's bearings taken around Avebury (Burl and Mortimer 2005, Appendix 2).[2] We can map these readings against known locations today and, allowing for the 4° of error of Stukeley's theodolite (Burl and Mortimer 2005: 152), the Beckhampton Avenue is noted on this sheet triangulated with many other extant features of the Avebury complex. Sixth, many archaeologists also doubted the existence of the Sanctuary until detailed use of Stukeley's testimony led to its rediscovery (Ucko 1991: 242).

In summary, multiple sources, documentary method, and logic enhance the validity of Stukeley's claim for a Fox Covert start/terminus for the Beckhampton Avenue against an overly skeptical professional archaeology.

Evidence from Field Survey

Field survey should expect less surviving evidence of stones for the Beckhampton Avenue compared to the West Kennet Avenue, since building stone would be in demand in the area where the village was built, west of the Avebury circle, compared to the uninhabited area around the West Kennet Avenue. Further west beyond the village along the claimed course of the Beckhampton avenue are racing horse stables and gallops, and their staff would have been directed to clear the area of hazardous sarsen stones.

Only a single pair of recumbent stones was recorded by Stukeley along the Beckhampton Avenue to the east of the Longstones enclosure.[3] Yet far more sarsen stones have been found or recorded in the area west of Longstones Cove on the route for the Beckhampton Avenue proposed by Twining and Stukeley, extending to Fox Covert. These are: two or more stones were reported to have been moved by Richard Fowler around 1700 at the crossroads of Calne Road and Field Way; Vatcher's stone of the 1969 excavation (Ucko et al. 1991:196); a stone is shown on the map on page 110 of Gillings et al. 2008 close to the A361, although not discussed in the text. The local antiquarian Pete Glastonbury has reported further stones around that area, many cleared from fields that the horses are exercised in so as not to risk these valuable animals: two stones on the Beckhampton road, one large one on the left by the small woods which may have been the covering stone that Faith Vatcher excavated in the 1960s when road works uncovered a child burial (SU 08549 68797); on the right of the road by the paddock and low down in the ditch is a triangular shaped stone which marked a gypsy grave (whiich used to be in the woods but was moved) at SU 08694 68877. In the stables is a pile of quite large sarsens in the garden in a heap which can only be seen in the winter months (reported to Pete Glastonbury by the jockeys in the Waggon & Horses public house); in the hedgerow behind The Grange there are two stones standing deep in the undergrowth that have been reused as an old gateway (SU 08669 69247); on the old Calne road is a buried stone which Stukeley was shown (SU 08339 69042); and in Beckhampton there are around thirty large stones used as garden ornaments, which probably came from "Chapel Field," close to the house now named "Silbury Court" (Pete Glastonbury: personal communication).

Although there may be some double-counting in this listing and, according to your assumptions on how many whole stones they may indicate, this adds up to between 8 and 40 possible stones on the route of the Beckhampton Avenue *to the south and west* of the Longstones Cove; that is, toward the direction of Fox Covert. Gillings et al. seem to be unaware of these further stones. But since the scarcity of stones east of the Longstones Cove was the basis for earlier archaeological rejections of the existence of the Beckhampton Avenue but which are now known to have existed, then more stones to the west of Longstones Cove *adds* weight to antiquarian reports that the Beckhampton Avenue extended further west. Gillings et al. discount these stones as being, variously: separate monuments; removed from avenue terminal at Longstones to mark outlying regions; abandoned from unfinished projects; mediaeval burial; sarsen-capped flat Beaker burial located close to Beckhampton spring (Gillings et al. 2008: 109). Pete Glastonbury sees the Beckhampton garden's stones not as avenue remains, but as collected from natural sarsen drift in Chapel Field, named after a chapel that once stood at the site of a house now named "Silbury Court."

These six additional theories to explain these extra stones, alongside the hypothesis of a short Beckhampton Avenue, are a more complicated alternative to the more parsimonious antiquarian testimony that all this evidence can be explained by a single Beckhampton Avenue continuing to Fox Covert.

Evidence of Geophysics Survey and Site Excavation

The geophysics survey carried out by Gillings et al. 50m to the south-west of the Longstones did not show any underground anomalies which might indicate buried stones or stone-holes. However, magnetometer and ground radar surveys frequently do not show underground features which exist because of variable soil and other conditions: "... the geophysical re-location of former stone settings can be particularly difficult, and is often of itself unable to provide unequivocal solutions" (Gillings et al. 2008: 11, 63, 67, 70, 103). Similarly, a geophysics survey of an area close to the Trusloe Cottages, midway between Longstones and the Avebury Circle, was expected to show traces of six stones, but actually showed possible traces for two. Subsequent excavation within this area instead revealed just one stone. Therefore instead of producing evidence for six stones the two methods combined showed definite evidence for only one—a failure rate against expectation of 83% (Gillings et al. 2008: 105). Even in this archaeologically most studied area, the enormous West Kennet Palisades just east of Silbury Hill were unknown until a full excavation had been carried out (Gillings et al. 2008: 3). Except for Vatcher's excavation which did find a sarsen buried near the Beckhampton roundabout, there has been little excavation of the remaining course of the Beckhampton Avenue claimed by Stukeley.

In 2003 a similar-sized trench was dug along a previously unexplored section of the West Kennet Avenue in a roughly symmetrical location to that of the Longstones enclosure. However, here also no trace of the West Kennet Avenue was found (Gillings et al. 2008: 139). The authors conclude that "... any assumption that the entire course of the Avenue comprised regular paired stone settings could represent a simplification of a more varied structural form." And "... the assumption of an unbroken line of stone pairs may not hold for the full length of both avenues." (Gillings et al. 2008: 103, 109 respectively). Since the West Kennet Avenue is known to extend to the Sanctuary another kilometer or so to the east, then it is as likely that the empty excavation just west of the Longstone enclosure is also a break in the continuity of an avenue that in fact extends further to the west, just as it does eastward past the gap in the West Kennet Avenue.

Evidence Anomalous to Theory

With the excavation of a 50m × 40m area to the south-west of the Longstones, "No stone-holes, stone destruction pits or stone burials were present, providing conclusive proof that the avenue did not continue in its known form beyond the Longstones Cove" (Gillings et al. 2008: 71). However, the phrase " in its known form " is inconsistent with "conclusive proof." If it did exist in another form, then it is "conclusive proof" of not much at all. And since we now know that its "form" included substantial gaps, then this statement is disingenuous. This inference is a consequence of Gillings and Pollard's "monuments as memory of ancient trackways model" (Gillings and Pollard 2004: 34 and 81). Such a model would find it hard to accommodate two avenues, unlike the one at Stonehenge, and would find it even harder to accommodate two discontinuous avenues. Instead of a rigorous testing of their own model, their conclusion for a short Beckhampton Avenue coupled with additional explanations for the many stones to the west of Longstones Cove could be seen as a *post hoc* adaptation to anomalous evidence.

If prehistoric stone avenues were a monumentalized memory of ancestral trackways, then it seems that culture-bearing modern humans first entered the Avebury area as Mesolithic hunter-gatherers along the Kennet Valley. From mappings of their base camps and extraction camps, Allen has shown their trackways would have included both the Kennet Valley and the dry valley which includes Fox Covert, but *not* the valley later followed by the West Kennet Avenue. Assuming that Gillings and Pollard allow their memory model to extend to the monument builders' Mesolithic ancestors, then Allen's work would predict that the Beckhampton Avenue, not West Kennet Avenue, would be remembered by later "lithicization" (Allen 2005). Perhaps it is the model, rather than the evidence, which is anomalous. Since memory also locks onto ritual and myth, not just ecological memory, then the monument builders' monumentalization of their forager memory may have required dispensing with the memory of their ancient trackways precisely to utilize those different parts of their local landscape which provided the best context for conducting their rituals and telling their myths. No Mesolithic sites were located on Windmill Hill, or the "occupation area" of West Kennet Avenue or the place of the Avebury circle. Yet these might have been exactly the right places to preserve aspects of that waning life for the cattle herders of the Neolithic/Early Bronze Age (EBA). Cosmological memory could, following this set of ethnographic assumptions, be best preserved by relocating monuments within a "new" landscape that evoked those myths to conduct rituals that were being adapted to and constitutive of their new circumstances.

Such an approach would overcome the now refuted "impediment" of a river crossing for a stone avenue. Rather than seeing rivers and wet places as a disadvantage to a processional way that monumentalized ancestral entry routes, it may well be that for initiatory journeys into a simulated underworld they were a preferred component of a monument complex (Sims 2009 and below). There is plenty of evidence for this hypothesis. The avenue at Stonehenge may well have been extended to the River Avon once the water table subsided below ground level at Stonehenge Bottom (Darvill 2007: 159); the Dorset Cursus was designed to descend into a marsh at the source of the River Allen (Tilley 1994: 184); and the longest stone row in the British Isles from Stall Moor to Green Hill in the Erme Valley on Dartmoor crosses the river and a large marshy triangular patch of red pebbles halfway along its 3.4km length (North 1996: 245–6; Sims 2003 field notes). Transit across or through a stretch of water or bog may well provide the digital alternation from wet to dry, such as provided by Beckhampton to West Kennet Avenues, which is a component of many initiation rituals. Burials where the Beckhampton Avenue crosses the River Winterbourne are additional signifiers to the metaphorical meaning of crossing a river into the underworld.

In an earlier publication, Gillings and Pollard found an indication of symmetry between the Beckhampton Avenue and the Ring Stone "extension" of the West Kennet Avenue as it approached the southern inner circle of the Avebury henge: "[I]t is interesting to note that the last [*sic*] stone pair of the Beckhampton Avenue before it entered the earlier enclosure also incorporated a perforated stone—an interesting symmetry perhaps?" (Gillings et al. 2004: 20). Interesting symmetry of a more substantial nature can be found between the Beckhampton and West Kennet Avenues:

1 The shapes and dimensions of the stones found buried in Beckhampton Avenue are the "same" as the stone shapes surviving in the West Kennet Avenue (Gillings et al. 2008: 5).

2 The average rectangular spacing of Beckhampton Avenue stones is 15m × 23m, and that of the West Kennet avenue is 17m × 24m (Gillings et al. 2008, 64).

3 The transverse stone L4 near the Longstones Cove (Gillings et al. 2008: 63) could be considered symmetrical to the transverse stone 35a in West Kennet Avenue, which is also about one-quarter the way along its route to the Sanctuary.

4 Part of the Gillings et al. justification for seeing the Longstones Cove as the terminus of the Beckhampton Avenue is that it is located alongside an early Neolithic/EBA "cemetery" on Folly Hill. By the same token, if EBA burial mounds are used to signify a symbolically potent part of the landscape, why discount Stukeley's claim of the Fox Covert, since that is also the location of another line of EBA burial mounds?

5 The Beckhampton Avenue passed directly through the Longstones east entrance "just as" the West Kennet avenue passed through the gap in the Occupation Area holes (Gillings et al.

2008: 81). But as the Occupation Area is within the length of the West Kennet Avenue, by making this observation of symmetry between the two avenues implies that the Longstones is also not a start/terminus point for the Beckhampton Avenue.

6 It could equally be argued that from its location alone that the Longstone's Cove and Folly Hill "cemetery" was a structure integrated into the course of a *longer* Beckhampton Avenue, just as Falkner's Circle is part of the way along the course of the West Kennet Avenue, or the King Barrow Ridge burial mounds are part of the Stonehenge Avenue midway along its length.

7 The concentration of lithics found around the Longstones Cove is echoed in the lithic concentration in the "Occupation Area" partway along the West Kennet Avenue.

8 The crouched inhumation burial at the Longstones Cove is on the north-east side of the "Adam" stone with its head to the south-east. West Kennet Avenue inhumation burials are also on the north-east side of the stones and for the one where there is evidence, the head was pointing to the south-west (Smith 1965: Plate 36a). Archaeologists have frequently identified cardinal and cross-cardinal alignments in prehistoric burials (Tuckwell 1975), and these alignments could only have been achieved by "astronomical" means. As there is a suggestion here of an orthogonal relationship between the two avenues' burials, then there may be grounds

for accepting an archaeoastronomical rationale of this lateral inversion in the symmetry of the Avenue "burials."

9 Behind the Sanctuary, which marks the "terminus" of the West Kennet Avenue, there is a line of barrows at right angles to the approaching avenue axis. But the line of the Folly Hill barrows, favored by Gillings and Pollard to mark the "terminus" of the Beckhampton Avenue, is parallel, not transverse, to the line of the avenue. However, at Fox Covert there is a linear barrow "cemetery" at right angles to the line of the Beckhampton Avenue as it "begins" its route to the Avebury Circle as suggested by Stukeley. If the principle of symmetry between the two avenues is accepted, then the Fox Covert barrows would be a better candidate for marking the start of the Beckhampton Avenue.

10 According to Stukeley, the West Kennet Avenue also had a cove about halfway along its length. If this were the case, then it would mirror the Longstones Cove along the Beckhampton Avenue, as a feature not signifying the terminus but an intermediate perhaps midway point along a longer Beckhampton Avenue. Stukeley described this other cove in detail, as a three-sided arrangement of stone pillars on the east side of the avenue opening out to the south-west "opposite one recumbent stone, two vacant stone positions and three fallen stones. Furthermore, at this point in the avenue, which he called the 'Apex,' he records that one of these Cove stones was 'carryed

away 1723' and another 'just buryed'." He also included a drawing of it in his panorama of the avenue. Ucko notes that "it is exactly this kind of apparently detailed evidence that has made it so difficult to discount Stukeley's claim for the existence of a Beckhampton avenue" (Ucko 1991: 190–3, also Plate 61). Since we now know that the Beckhampton Avenue existed, then perhaps a more appropriate rule would be that wherever Stukeley provides "detailed evidence," as is the case with the West Kennet Avenue cove, we should strive to conduct exhaustive tests rather than prematurely doubt his testimony. Gillings and Pollard suggest that if the cove existed it would now be buried beneath the modern road, so that Stukeley's claim cannot be tested (Gillings and Pollard 2004: 20). However, it may be that the West Kennet Avenue cove was located in a position which can be tested. According to Pete Glastonbury the West Kennet cove was 70m north of the existing stone on the west side of the road, or where stone pair 50 should be, assuming average spacing. From field survey in that position is a flat, high area of ground with clear horizon views all round, just as the Longstones and northern inner circle coves are positioned on local raised ground. This position is confirmed by Stukeley's triangulation data in the Cardiff library source mentioned above, and therefore the West Kennet Avenue cove's existence may be testable.

These ten pieces of evidence for symmetrical form and properties between the two avenues strengthens the case for extending symmetry to their length and course, which in turn indicates the start/terminus for Beckhampton Avenue at Fox Covert (North 1996: 248–64).

Evidence from Theoretical Pluralism

Facts become "facts" when they are predicted by theory. A "processions" perspective which views avenues as monumental reminders of ancestral transit routes would find it difficult to accommodate duplication and discontinuity into their design and would also minimize the significance of local landscape features that might be appropriated for ritual purposes. However, other theories can. Cleal has demonstrated a frequent association between monuments and bourne holes, or seasonally-occurring watercourses, which "might have appeared mysterious, liminal, a reminder of the forces inhabiting the landscape and only intermittently apparent … [I]n the Beckhampton Road 'dry valley' … [d]uring the wet winters of the 1990s and the early 21st century the northern part of the valley had rising ground water extending from south-west of the junction of the Roman road with the present road … Lining this stretch of valley are concentrations of round barrows, including linear settings, *particularly at Fox Covert* …" (Cleal 2005: 122, my emphasis). The ritual amplification of the periodic emergence of water from underground by constructing an avenue which "starts" at Fox Covert is consistent with seeing the Avebury complex as intended to simulate a journey into and returning from the underworld (Sims 2009).

Stukeley noticed that the Avebury monuments were organized in a highly paradoxical arrangement: "every part is hid from the other or but obscurely visible …" (Ucko et al. 1991: 84). When we submit these digital alternations between obscured and "obscurely visible," we find that the course of the two avenues prescribe horizon views of the upper terrace of Silbury Hill from only five positions, and are designed to disallow all other viewing for nearly 80 percent of their length—from Fox Covert; the Beckhampton Avenue where it crosses the River Winterbourne; the Avebury Circle cove; the "D" feature; and the Sanctuary. Seeing the top terrace as a sliver of scoured chalk, these views allow the Silbury Hill summit to be perceived as crescent moon before and after dark moon at the winter solstice. From two positions, at the River Winterbourne and at the Sanctuary, the Silbury Hill summit is perfectly in line with the background horizon. There could not be a more dramatic signifier of the moon when it has set. It would be apparent to prehistoric participants in ritual processions in the Avebury monuments that only from the underworld can the moon be seen when it has set. In particular, as can be seen in Fig 2, while the Beckhampton Avenue is shown by Stukeley as a track with few stones, at its "start" it points directly to the Silbury Hill summit proud of its background eastern horizon, which is the only direction in which waning crescent moon can be observed, and the line of sight follows the line of the flow of water as it periodically emerges from the underground at exactly that spot. Discontinuous water flows, and digital alternation between dark- and new-moon rituals timed to coincide with the solstices, if reflected in the monument design, would then explain duplication and discontinuity in avenue arrangements. Since these different theories predict very different properties for the avenues, the scholarly procedure in testing your preferred theory is to always test the critical opposing theory. It is surprising that Gillings et al. do not suggest further exploratory geophysics and trenches in the area around and to the east of Fox Covert.

Concluding Comments

This note is not intended to advocate an uncritical attitude to Stukeley's testimony (see Ucko et al. 1991: 157 and passim). It may be the case that Gillings et al. are correct in their view of a short Beckhampton Avenue. But that case won't stand with these arguments. Scholarship moves forward by attempting to refute hypotheses comprehensively. Since field walking for stones, geophysics, and one short trench excavation cannot provide guaranteed tests to Twinings and Stukeley's claim for a Fox Covert start/terminus to the Beckhampton Avenue, other tests are required. By antiquarian and folk testimony, divided opinion among current scholars, direct evidence of stone remains, differential processes of monument destruction, inconsistent evaluation of Stukeley's testimony, the unreliability of geophysics survey, logically inconsistent argumentation, the complexity of the Avebury avenues' architecture, substantial evidence for symmetrical properties and arrangements between the two Avebury avenues, the evident integration of local landscape

features (particularly water) with monument layout, and lunar-solar conflation theory—all of these account for twenty-four reasons which attest to the *probability* that the Beckhampton Avenue did extend beyond the Longstones. Whether it continued intermittently, marked with stones or posts or just as a path, is not considered by Gillings et al. An open and multidisciplinary research agenda should not be forestalled by a premature closure of this probability.

Acknowledgements
With thanks to Pete Glastonbury, Steve Marshall, and Neil Mortimer for comments on an earlier draft of this paper.

Notes

1 See Gillings et al. 2008 for full list of references on all these and other features.

2 With thanks to Neil Mortimer for pointing out this source to me.

3 Others have been found by Pete Glastonbury as foundation stones for the River Winterbourne bridge: http://www.peteglastonbury.plus.com/Apod/Apod30.htm

References

Allen, S., 2005. "Mesolithic Hunter-gatherer Exploitation of the Marlborough Downs." in G. Brown, D. Field, and David McOmish (eds), *The Avebury Landscape: Aspects of the Field Archaeology of the Marlborough Downs*. Oxford: Oxbow, pp. 95–102.

Burl, A., 2002. *Prehistoric Avebury*. London: Yale University Press.

Burl, A. and Mortimer, N. (eds), 2005. *Stukeley's Stonehenge: an Unpublished Manuscript*. London: Yale University Press.

Cleal, R., 2005. "'The small compass of a grave:' Early Bronze Age Burial in and around Avebury and the Marlborough Downs." in G. Brown, D. Field, and David McOmish (eds), *The Avebury Landscape: Aspects of the Field Archaeology of the Marlborough Downs*. Oxford: Oxbow, pp. 115–32.

Darvill, T., 2007. *Stonehenge: The Biography of a Landscape*. Stroud: Tempus.

Gillings, M. and Pollard, D., 2004. *Avebury*. London: Duckworth.

Gillings, M., Pollard, J., and Wheatley, D.W., 2000. "The Beckhampton Avenue and a 'new' Neolithic Enclosure near Avebury: an Interim Report on the 1999 Excavations." *Wiltshire Archaeological Magazine* 93: 1–8.

Gillings, M., Pollard, J., Wheatley, D., and Peterson, R., 2008. *Landscape of the Megaliths: Excavation and Fieldwork on the Avebury Monuments, 1997–2003*. Oxford: Oxbow Books.

Malone, C., 1989. *English Heritage Book of Avebury*. London: Batsford.

Mortimer, N., 2003. *Stukeley Illustrated: William Stukeley's Rediscovery of Britain's Ancient Sites*. Sutton Mallet: Green Magic.

North, J., 1996. *Stonehenge: Neolithic Man and Cosmos*. London: HarperCollins.

Peterson, R., 2003. "Thomas Twining's Roman Avebury." *Wiltshire Studies* 96: 210–13.

Sims, L.D., 2009. "Entering, and Returning from, the Underworld: Reconstituting Silbury Hill by Combining a Quantified Landscape Phenomenology with Archaeoastronomy." *Journal of the Royal Anthropological Institute* 15:2, 386–408.

Smith, I., 1965. *Windmill Hill and Avebury: Excavations by Alexander Keiller 1925–1939*. Oxford: Clarendon.

Tilley, C., 1994. *A Phenomenology of Landscape*. Oxford: Berg.

Tuckwell, A.N., 1975. "Patterns of Burial Orientation in the Round Barrows of East Yorkshire." Bulletin of the Institute of Archaeology, University of London 12 (1975): 95–123.

Ucko, P.J., Hunter, M., Clark, A.J., and David, A., 1991. *Avebury Reconsidered: From the late 1660s to the 1990s*. London: Unwin Hyman.

**Time and Mind:
The Journal of
Archaeology,
Consciousness
and Culture**

Volume 2—Issue 3
November 2009
pp. 347–348

DOI:
10.2752/175169609X12464529903254

Reprints available directly
from the publishers

Photocopying permitted by
license only

Correspondence

The Editors reserve the right to edit letters if necessary for space or other relevant reasons.

Rock Art: "Tatooing" Rocks?

Robert J. Wallis's perceptive article on "Re-enchanting Rock Art Landscapes" (T&M 2:1, pp. 47–70) constitutes a welcome attempt to step out of the straitjacket of post-Cartesian materialist/rationalist approaches to the interpretation of the monuments of prehistory. As a nonspecialist, nevertheless fascinated by what might be called the Religious Studies element of the understanding of prehistory, I am moved to suggest an analogy which might usefully further illuminate Wallis's argument. This is the practice of tattooing, the marking of human persons with permanent patterns and/or figurative art, usually at the hands of another person in some sense a professional in the production of body art.

We know that such body art was current in prehistoric times, for example on the preserved remains of a Neolithic hunter ("Oetzi") found in the Austrian Alps in 1991 (Spindler 1995: 167–73). A range of meanings for the practice at that time have been suggested, including therapeutic activities and the representation of events in the life of the recipient. The more obvious functions of adornment and expressing aspects of personality or emotions must not be overlooked either. (My own experience of friendship with a Texan prison inmate confirms that such motives still lie behind the reception of tattoos in modern Western culture: his tattoos include representations of his anger at incarceration, his feelings about his country and the date of his recapture after escape, as well as "Celtic-style" abstract adornment with no deeper meaning.) My point is that in tattooing we have a practice in which the production of the art is done at the wish of the recipient but at the hands of another: in a modern context, the primary, voluntary agency of the recipient initiates the production of the art, while the skill and physical exertion of the artist is secondary to this agency. Considering Rock Art through an animic worldview might lead one to conceive that a similar transaction was at work: the other-than-human person of the rock-face initiates the production of art through the skills and efforts of the human artist, perhaps through dreams or other metaphysical communications. A glimpse of the kind of experience which might give rise to the production of Rock Art is afforded by Genesis 28:10–22, in which, following a dream, Jacob "took the stone that he had put for his pillows, and set it up for a pillar, and poured oil upon the top of it." In this story from the Bronze Age Near East, beneath the later monotheistic editing, it is noticeable that Jacob is recognizing and responding to the already existing nonhuman persons of the place: "Surely [the Lord] is in this place; and I knew it not," and it is this recognition that leads him to mark out the place as sacred and liminal for future human visitors.

The value that the analogy of tattooing might add to our understanding of Rock Art consists, in part, of the reflection that tattooing may often express existing characteristics of the recipients while at the same time subtly changing what is, by expressing it. It locks a particular moment into a longer-lasting "present." Recipients may grow to regret their decision to invite such permanent markings: the meanings they sought to express may be reinterpreted as their attitudes and feelings develop. Tattooing can also bring into being new aspects of a recipient's personality, for example by reifying imagined or aspired-to character traits. The applicability of these considerations to Rock Art, too, may, I hope, help us to enter more fully into the animic mindset in which the art was generated.

More generally, Wallis's article encourages speculation as to whether Rock Art was part of a wider range of phenomena which could not be so easily reconstructed by archaeological investigation: was the tattooing of the rock people accompanied by cognate patterning of the broader landscape? Is this echoed in the British tradition of the cutting of chalk figures and mazes in the turf? Certainly, the living and peopled nature of the Neolithic landscape must have been expressed through the kind of movement, dance, music, art, and audience engagement so movingly described by Yvette Staelens elsewhere in your pages as taking place at the "Enclosure" event at Hambledon Hill (T&M 2:1, pp. 119–24). To engage meaningfully with Rock Art, we all need to keep in mind that what remains of prehistory was only a part of a far greater—and no doubt to modern rationalist minds a far stranger—nexus of ideas, practices and events which now are only accessible to imagination and guesswork.

Paul Kitchenham
Bexhill-on-Sea, England

Reference

Spindler, K., 1995. *The Man in the Ice*. London: Phoenix.

**Time and Mind:
The Journal of
Archaeology,
Consciousness
and Culture**

Volume 2—Issue 3
November 2009
pp. 349–350
DOI:
10.2752/175169609X12464529903290

Reprints available directly
from the publishers

Photocopying permitted by
license only

Correspondence

Seeing the Light

Thank you for publishing the thorough and excellent
article by Dr. Euan MacKie on the prehistoric calendar and
the evidence of prehistoric astronomical interest that has
continued to accumulate since Professor Thom's death. I hope
that gradually more prehistorians will realize that Professor
Thom's rejected theories are the only way forward out of the
present cul-de-sac in the subject.

Professor Thom's discoveries about ancient astronomy,
measurement, and geometry are quietly being validated all
over the country by the few students of prehistory who are
prepared to develop the necessary skills. Close to where I live
here in Wales, for instance, at a prehistoric site unknown to
either Professor Thom or Dr. MacKie, there is clear evidence
that the site was located with reference to the sky (solar
and lunar cycles as well as north/south alignments), that the
megalithic yard was the unit of measurement used, and that
the cairns were designed by careful geometry. The problem
is not that the evidence is lacking but that archaeologists are
not trained to see it.

I would also like to add that it is easy to forget the extent
of sea travel in prehistory, for which a precise knowledge
of the sky for navigational purposes on the open sea would
have been a matter of life or death. If people could sail long
distances by observing the stars, sun, and moon, then it is not
surprising that they used the same skills and knowledge when
locating their monuments on land.

Irene Earis
Pantyfedwen, Wales

Time and Mind:
The Journal of
Archaeology,
Consciousness
and Culture

Volume 2—Issue 3
November 2009
pp. 351–354

DOI:
10.2752/175169609X12464529903335

Book Review

The Archaeology of Semiotics and the Social Order of Things

George Nash and George Children, eds

Archaeopress, 2008
Pb, 204pp. ISBN: 9781407303178

Reviewed by Barry Lewis

This edited volume of fifteen papers in the British Archaeological Reports series sets out to convince the reader that grammar and signs can be teased out and described from archaeological landscapes. Semiotics can often be a daunting subject on which to write and sometimes even more daunting to read, with authors failing to engage fully with the nature of the subject matter and in turn failing to engage the reader. So it was with some (mild) trepidation that I read this new offering. However, right from the introductory chapter this collection was engaging and thought provoking. Nash and Children set out their stall well, and give us a clear direction about where their book is heading. Along the way there were a few little stumbles but nothing that detracted from either the theme or the book's overall achievements in giving some clarity to this emerging area of archaeological thought. Semiotics and structuralist thought have been insinuating their way into other disciplines for the past three decades or so, especially in literature and particularly in literary criticism. It was Nash who first applied this thinking to archaeology in 1997 in *Semiotics and Landscape: Archaeology of Mind*, another edited volume.

The contributors discuss landscapes from all points of the compass within Europe, North America, and Australia, and there is even an unusual but illuminating account by Thomas Heyd of a seventeenth-century travel diary by the Japanese poet Matsuo Bashō. Naturally enough, given the editors' research interests, there are seven papers on rock art and its associated landscapes, with others touching on the subject to a lesser degree. Given that semiotics is very much the "science of signs" it seems an entirely appropriate weighting.

Good use of primary data is made in Matthew Kelleher's paper on stone arrangements in the Blue Mountains of Australia, just to the west of Sydney. His analysis points convincingly to an articulation of landscape features, accented by the placement of stone arrangements, which were perhaps used as shrines or waymarks in an acculturated landscape. Manuel Estévez uses excavations in Galicia (northwest Spain) to suggest that the chronology of this stylistic assemblage of Atlantic rock art can be stretched further into later prehistory, by some 2,500 years.

Some papers combine theoretical and empirical approaches to show us the practice of semiotics in the landscape. This is the approach which Paul Devereux explores through the use of archaeoacoustics as a feature of rock-art landscapes in North America, Wales, and other parts of the world. He shows how soundscape affected the selection of sites for rock marking, a method of study which has previously been underused and poorly understood. These differing approaches become focused through the use of semiotics and demonstrate how the tangible and the intangible elements of landscape and rock art can come together to offer new narratives and to articulate a grammar of landscape.

Clegg writes about his recent research in a chapter on "landscape, semiotics, and rock-art in Ku-Ring-Gai Chase." This peninsula, just to the north of Sydney in Broken Bay, is a place that I am also familiar with. Clegg's work could be interesting but suffers from inadequate explanation and poor illustrations—he also repeats the cumbersome (and pointless) word "snames" for dish-like depressions in the local rock. Some of the highlights of the paper, such as an exploration of a phenomenological approach to the site, are too tentative. This particular section, in which he describes the experience of moving around the site, offers an obviously phenomenological approach, though Clegg does not use the term or even qualify his method.

Angelo Fossati's chapter is titled "Following Arianna's Thread" (he means Ariadne's thread, something the editors do not seem to have registered). He looks at Valcamonica and gives a succinct introduction to the region's rock art before embarking on a well-argued case for the presence of a rock art made by or relevant to the interests of women, predating the male-dominated Iron Age motifs. Kalle Sognnes examines the late Mesolithic and Neolithic assemblages of rock-art engravings from Central Norway, and compares them to the use of symbols on items of material culture, such as spearheads, which may have been used as signals of ethnicity. He also suggests that these symbolic systems may reflect shamanistic behaviors, and that these could have been used to define ethnicity more clearly.

An interesting chapter takes a more psychological or philosophical approach to the questions posed by a structuralist view of our relationship with landscape. Merritt's discussion argues for a Jungian "ecopsychological perspective" in viewing sacred landscapes. It provides an interesting insight into how psychologists view the human relationship with landscape as an object within the human psyche. Human notions of sacred landscapes and their attendant rituals are explained as part of a package of wonder and awe at the continuing pattern of life and death in a world of deep psychological meaning tied to special places and ceremonies. This is a short chapter, and it rushes through some key areas which are worthy of further explanation or examination.

A chapter by Skeie takes us back to Norway, this time to the east of the country for an examination of the "experience of rock-art" and a look at the repetition of symbols in different parts of the landscape considering what might be encoded in their meaning and how as researchers we should approach the rock art today. Skeie concludes that the art, particularly deer motifs, was perceived in the Mesolithic by hunters in ways that depended upon the season and the carvings' location within the landscape, and that perceptions changed over time. She points out that our lack of familiarity with some of the places we study, coming to them invariably as visitors from elsewhere, means that we miss some crucial aspects of the meaning encoded into rock art. In the penultimate chapter Nash takes a look at Neolithic burial monuments along Strumble Head, reviewing their linear position within the landscape and their placement among jagged peaks. In general this commentary provides a thought-provoking look at the depth of time during which such monuments were used and the way in which burial practices and monument architecture subtly changed over that time.

All in all, this is an interesting and engaging book and one that contributes much to an emerging discipline within archaeology that should, I hope, stimulate more work and debate about these approaches and interpretations.

**Time and Mind:
The Journal of
Archaeology,
Consciousness
and Culture**

Volume 2—Issue 3
November 2009
pp. 355–358
DOI:
10.2752/175169609X12464529903371

Book Review

Belief in the Past: Theoretical Approaches to the Archaeology of Religion

David S. Whitely and Kelley Hays-Gilpin, eds

Left Coast Press, 2008
Pb, 289pp. ISBN: 9781598743425

Reviewed by Anthony Aveni

Belief in the Past is a collection of discussions by art historians, anthropologists, and archaeologists about how one goes about acquiring a knowledge of religious behavior in past and present cultures (among them the Venda, Viking, Mississippian, Ojibwa, and Pueblo) that offer little or no textual evidence to supply this knowledge. Reading it, I was surprised to discover clear parallels between the development of the archaeology of religion (call it "archaeoreligion") and archaeoastronomy, or the study of the practice of astronomy of cultures other than our own gleaned from the study of the unwritten record, principally from archaeology.

Just as the other organized disciplines have delayed serious engagement with the study of past religions, so the science that existed in the past has long been ignored or misinterpreted. This ignorance lasted until the 1960s, when rigorous methodologies were developed and questions were formulated about the diverse relationships between people and sky—questions that began to make sense to historians of culture. As was the case when the interdisciplinary engagement with ethnoscience became serious, and led to modifications of the definition of science, so likewise the study of archaeoreligion makes it clear that the manifestation of spirituality in past societies bears no relationship to our modern understanding of this concept. This is a feature of several chapters in this book, among them Price's article on "Bodylore and the archaeology of embedded religion."

The book opens with four theoretical chapters that deal with the several definitions of religion and the questions of where it comes from, how and why it changes, how it operates in society, what relation there is between emotion and reason, the nature of religious metaphor, and the recognition that religion has a substantive character of its own and is not a mere epiphenomenon of other social practices. Explanatory models are proposed to explore the cognitive mechanisms involved in our religious predilections and the issue of whether religion is a product of human evolution—are we hardwired for it? These well-integrated chapters, dealing with basic concepts and questions about systems of belief, might well be read quite apart from the rest of the book.

There follows a series of chapters on three basic subject areas. First, there are the metaphysical aspects of religion such as one finds in certain forms of Buddhism and in shamanism. The piece by Whitely on "Cognition, emotion, and belief" argues that emotion and reason are coeval and rooted in neural development. A second group of chapters focuses on theory and practice of more concrete aspects of religion, such as ceremonial architecture and funerary practice. One realizes that to understand the role of religion in daily life, one needs to look beyond the elite goods which are so often the focus of archaeological investigations. Finally, there is

the role of the landscape: water, mountains, shrines. These latter two broad subject areas emphasize the embeddedness of religious practice in daily life. I found Scarre's piece on "Shrines of the hand and places of power" particularly fascinating. It engages the oft-unexplored subject of the anthropomorphization of monumental stone. His discussion of the megalithic monuments finds echoes in the practice in other cultures, such as the Inca of Cuzco, who view their sacred stones and even their mountains as living ancestors.

The final chapters of the book are shaped around the contribution which can be made to the study of past beliefs by the contemporary ethnographic record. Here the subject matter includes gender among the Pueblo and the Australian Aborigines, the behaviour of Siberian hunter-gatherers, and the ritual practice of contemporary Ojibwa. And so, back to the parallel: ethnoreligion is rendered a part of all aspects of social practice. You cannot isolate it for separate study.

Though there is a good dose of archaeological material in this work, I wish there had been more. Rock art is one of the categories of archaeological evidence with which the authors engage, but this is always problematic, and like religion is often marginalized by the archaeologist. The contributors also deal with the analysis of burial goods and practices, and with the layout of ceremonial centers, especially their relation to cosmological principles in such recurrent forms as dualism and quadripartition. Emerson and Pauketat's chapter on "Historical-processual archaeology and culture making" is particularly illuminating on this.

It's to be hoped that this strongly theoretical text will be given the wide disciplinary readership it deserves, and will go a long way toward bringing religion back in from the margins as something to be considered in the study of the material record.

**Time and Mind:
The Journal of
Archaeology,
Consciousness
and Culture**

Volume 2—Issue 3
November 2009
pp. 359–362

DOI:
10.2752/175169609X12464529903416

Reprints available directly
from the publishers

Photocopying permitted by
license only

Book Review

Archaeology is a Brand: The Meaning of Archaeology in Contemporary Popular Culture

Cornelius Holtorf

Archaeopress 2007
Pb, 184 pp. ISBN 9781905739066

Reviewed by Bob Trubshaw

If, as the truism goes, the past only exists in the present
moment, then archaeology as a discipline should sit firmly
within the realms of contemporary culture. This is manifestly
not the case. But fear not, Holtorf is not arguing for
archaeology to be seen as a subset of cultural studies. Instead,
his aims are spread throughout the book in a number of
evolving statements. Initially he writes: "This book is about the
meaning of archaeology in contemporary popular culture. It
is not a manual for improving the public understanding of the
discipline of archaeology." He goes on to specifically exclude
what might be expected: "This book is … *not* about how
professional archaeologists themselves see their own subject."
Only as far into the book as page 61 are we told that "this
work's focus is on attitudes about archaeology as reflected
in popular culture." And further on we are given another
clue: "The full title of the project of which this book is the
outcome was 'The portrayal of archaeology in contemporary
popular culture—opportunity or obstacle for the promotion
of cultural heritage?'." By the time Holtorf draws some
conclusions from his investigations, he also illuminates his
objectives more succinctly. "The most important question that
archaeologists in public contexts need to ask their audiences
is not 'How can I best persuade you about the merits of my
project or discipline?' but 'What does what I am doing mean
to you?'."

The absence of a clear opening "objective" requires this book to be quickly skimmed for its key ideas before a detailed understanding can be attempted. Understandably and inevitably, it also requires familiarity with Holtorf's previous and wider-ranging study of archaeology and popular culture, *From Stonehenge to Las Vegas: Archaeology as Popular Culture* (Altamira 2005).

The initial quick skim will reveal some detailed evaluations of how archaeology appears in the popular culture of Britain, Germany, and Sweden. These three countries are those most familiar to the author. Despite approaching them in an open-minded manner, Holtorf soon concludes that the only significant difference between the portrayal of archaeology in the three nations is the outstanding success of *Time Team* in Britain. Other than that, archaeology achieves similar "presence" and TV audience figures—and those audience figures are often quite substantial. (In Britain this means that *Time Team* has attained similar viewing figures as *Big Brother*, i.e., 10 to 15 percent of the viewing public.) Holtorf's studies look only at mass-circulation newspapers, and largely ignore magazines. So *British Archaeology* gets only a passing mention and *Current Archaeology* is ignored. This is consistent with the author's studies which confirm what might reasonably be expected, that "the single most significant source of information about archaeology is TV."

Although the number of archaeological documentaries is surprisingly high (Holtorf suggesting about two a day—including repeats—on British TV schedules in 2001), this is far from the total archaeological content of broadcasting. From blockbuster films such as the Indiana Jones trilogy down to bit parts in assorted dramas, archaeologists pop up frequently. More especially, the past is everywhere in TV and advertising. Relics of ancient people are encountered in the branding of countless products and services. And on top of all the TV diggers there is one more fictional archaeologist who cannot be ignored—Lara Croft.

Fictionalized archaeologists such as Jones, Croft, and a host of additional characters in novels, B-movies and the like are, for Holtorf, not an epiphenomenon but a key to understanding how archaeology is perceived by the public. Most importantly, they have given archaeologists one of the best public images of any profession. "Few disciplines are lucky enough to be similarly widely and similarly positively represented in popular culture as archaeology is. The brand of archaeology is associated with so many positive appeals, stories, and dreams that other brands, despite their sometimes vast advertising budgets, can only envy … one could hardly imagine archaeology's image to be more favorable than it already is."

Yet most professional archaeologists are uncomfortable with these associations. "It simply astonishes me that a fairly large proportion of archaeologists still seem to find nothing more urgent than to distance themselves from popular heroes like Indiana Jones or Lara Croft. It is deeply ironic that nothing seems to be harder for archaeologists to get to grips with in their relations with non-archaeologists than their seemingly limitless and virtually untainted overall popularity that is unrivalled among academic disciplines."

This feeling of misperception runs deeper, notes Holtorf. "For many archaeologists the key issue in this context appears to be that they feel fundamentally misrepresented regarding the depiction of both the existing knowledge about the past and their own occupation."

One of the strengths of *Archaeology is a Brand* is the contrast which it draws between the aims of most professional archaeologists and the way in which archaeology is perceived and consumed by the public. Leisure pursuits are increasingly sold as experiences, with these experiences selling dreams and fairytale narratives. This "experience industry" is "first and foremost about *engaging* people sensually, cognitively, socially, culturally and emotionally." Again, archaeology is well-placed to offer just such as experiences, as the Jorvik Centre in York has amply demonstrated, although Jorvik remains the exception rather than the norm.

Emotional stories and narratives about the past have, of course, been with us for considerable time. They include stories about nations, political ideologies, and state religions. Although few archaeologists are proud of it, in the past they too "have been making significant contributions to each of these grand stories … Only recently has a focus on *national* heritage been replaced by one on the *cultural* heritage."

Fantasy adventure is an ever-increasing aspect of marketing, and one in which "archaeology seems pre-destined to play a key role." In part this is because the best-known archaeological narratives have a strong sense of adventure, discovery, and "revelation." Holtorf pertinently draws in a quotation from John Fritz's writings from back in 1973 when he states: "The reason

why archaeologists should have special access to such great truths goes beyond their ability to solve mysteries and recover treasures … the archaeologist is 'an intermediary between the worldly and the other worldly and between the quick and the dead'. In as much as it is possible to bring lost civilisations back to life and make ancient artefacts speak, terms often used to describe archaeology, it involves supernatural powers and achieves true miracles" (citing Fritz 1973: 6).

Holtorf goes beyond merely itemizing the representation of archaeologists and "the past" in popular culture. His analysis identifies four main themes in the way archaeologists are presented in popular culture—as Adventurer, Detective and scholar, Source of profound revelations, or Caretaker/conservator.

These four themes share certain aspects. Significantly, in none of them is the archaeologist portrayed "in relation to his actual ability to find out what happened in the past but [instead] in relation to certain qualities that are associated with this basic ambition … In none of these four themes are the actual results of archaeological work particularly important. Instead, what matters most are various aspects of the process of doing archaeology." This is of course in common with the typical adventure or detective story.

"What all four themes share too, is their emphasis on archaeology as a process, that is 'doing' archaeology rather than on the actual results being produced." Far more emphasis is given to how archaeologists arrive at any given insight than to the insight itself. "The most common association people have with 'archaeology' is invariably the notion of digging up things"—although *Time*

Team has added "geofizz" to this popular perception.

Alongside these perceived roles of the archaeologist, Holtorf considers that the public role of archaeology as a discipline can be thought of as fitting into three dominant categories:

1 educational, through presenting "proper archaeology" in opposition to populist archaeology;
2 public relations, through presenting the overall aims of archaeology in a politically, economically, and socially favorable manner; and, most contentiously,
3 democratic, through requiring professionals to change according to what people actually want from archaeology.

Both the educational and PR models suffer from their limited applicability to specific sections of society. They are simply too exclusive and assume that once people are told the "right" way then they will automatically want to follow. But the way archaeology is depicted in popular culture overwhelmingly confirms that this is not the case. For example, Graham Hancock and Robert Bauval command much bigger TV audiences than "proper" Egyptologists. What people want from archaeology is often contrary to what professional archaeologists are naturally disposed to provide. Where is the middle ground? And how can archaeologists best adapt to the public's wants? Holtorf offers little in the way of guidance. But then he specifically stated that he was not offering a manual for improving the public understanding of archaeology.

Holtorf has succeeded in researching and analysing a crucial—yet hitherto ignored—aspect of archaeology. His examples are revelatory and his discussion is astute. However, the main accomplishment of this book lies in something that does not appear within its pages—its ability to generate awareness of these crucial issues among the archaeological profession. Here's hoping that archaeology in contemporary popular culture now begins to build on the small number of outstanding successes.

References

Fritz, J., 1973. "Relevance, Archaeology and Subsistence Theory." in C. Redman (ed.), *Research and Theory in Current Archaeology*. New York: John Wiley & Sons.

Holtorf, C., 2005. *From Stonehenge to Las Vegas: Archaeology as Popular Culture*. Walnut Creek, CA: AltaMira Press.

Time and Mind:
The Journal of
Archaeology,
Consciousness
and Culture

Volume 2—Issue 3
November 2009
pp. 363–366

DOI:
10.2752/175169609X12464529903335

Book Review

Theorizing Religions Past: Archaeology, History, and Cognition

Harvey Whitehouse and Luther H. Martin, eds

AltaMira, 2004
Pb, 262pp. ISBN 9780759106215

Reviewed by Robert J. Wallis

The thirteen chapters in *Theorizing Religions Past* (part of Alta Mira's "Cognitive Science of Religion" series, also edited by Whitehouse and Martin) are the result of a 2002 international conference held at the University of Vermont. At this gathering, archaeologists, classicists, historians, and historians of religion came together to assess the "modes of religiosity" theory which had been proposed by Whitehouse in his ethnography of the Baining of Papua New Guinea, *Inside the Cult*. Whitehouse's theory proposes two modes of religiosity, the "doctrinal" and the "imagistic," proposed at first as a specific response to the ethnography of the Baining, but afterward recognized as having value for examining human religiosity more widely. Whitehouse argues that a cluster of variables characterize each mode. In the doctrinal mode, there would be a "digital" or discursive style of recording often characteristic of literate societies, a transmission of beliefs by routinized instruction and repetitive ritual, and a wide dissemination of tradition among communities with largely anonymous group affinities. In the imagistic mode, we would expect an "analogic" or imagistic style of codification, and this would be transmitted through infrequently performed rituals rendered memorable through intense sensory, emotionally charged ritual among cohesive, small-scale communities. Memory and transmission themselves are differently constituted in each mode, through media varying from the generalized scripts or schemas of the doctrinal to the episodic or autobiographical mechanisms of the imagistic.

The variety of chapters scrutinize the efficacy of the theory in a range of contexts, from prehistory through the Graeco-Roman period to medieval and eighteenth-century Christianity. Through their analysis of these very different contexts, the authors are able to use Whitehouse's theory with greater subtlety than it had at its first appearance, suggesting that the "modes of religiosity" approach can achieve a certain theoretical purchase. The interdisciplinarity of the discussions—which span psychology, anthropology, archaeology, and history—signals a welcome cross-fertilization and demonstrates the benefits for scholars of engaging with one another's theoretical considerations. But it is disappointing that, despite this interdisciplinarity, only two of the thirteen chapters attend to prehistory. A further three examine Classical religion and four focus on Christianity. Four seems rather too many; perhaps this period was preferred because Whitehouse's doctrinal mode seems more evident in that era than in others. The final two chapters (one by Whitehouse himself) offer some theoretical discussion.

The most interesting chapters are "From Ohala to Çatalhöyük" by Mithen, which engages with the early prehistory of Western Asia, and "Corrupt doctrine and doctrinal revival" in which Pyysiäinen examines the Laestadian movement in Finland during the latter half of the nineteenth century. These two discussions test Whitehouse's theory in relation to the most ancient and the most recent instances of religion covered in the book.

Mithen's chapter examines archaeological evidence for religiosity in western Asia from 20,000 to 7,000 BC, not "as a formal test of anthropological theory regarding religion" but to offer a 'longer-term perspective on how religiosity develops in relation to economy and society than is possible from the ethnographic record alone." At first glance this longer-term view might seem to sit well with the theory of the two modes, as an economic shift from hunting and gathering to farming might broadly be said to be accompanied by a move from imagistic to more doctrinal religions. Mithen argues, however, that for most of the period the religious mode was imagistic and so the term is "far too gross to be of potential value." Further, he sees the distinction between imagistic and doctrinal as "too coarse to be of value to prehistoric archaeologists," suggesting that diversity should not be overlooked and that before the theory is applied to prehistoric evidence, the existence of "patterned variation" in ethnographic contexts needs to be addressed.

Pyysiäinen explores how the Swedish Lutheran priest Laestadius argued against enlightenment philosophy, with it modernization of religion and "rationalist theology." He turned instead to a "religion of the heart" and the value of each individual's personal spiritual experience. He preached temperance to the Sami at a time when the alcohol sold to them by settlers was causing immense social problems, and argued against doctrinal innovations in the Church, which he saw as a degeneration. The practice of *liikutus* ('being moved'—spontaneous and uncontrolled expressions of emotion) was an important part of the Laestadian movement and this, along with some Sami ancestry, perhaps informed his interest in shamanism. Certainly such signs of *liikutus* as "laughing, hiccoughing, and imitations of animal voices" as well as "jumping and swinging around," shaking, convulsing, and falling to the ground, are all reminiscent of the performances of shamans. Pyysiäinen argues that Whitehouse's theory was coined to explain "regularities in traditions," so that it is "not particularly helpful" in addressing such inspirational or imagistic practices as *liikutus* and the other elements which gave dynamism to the Laestadian critique of doctrinal Lutheranism.

Whitehouse and Martin's book has a somewhat misleading title, since it focuses on the modes theory, applied primarily to historic religions, and does not deal with "theorizing religions past" or with "archaeology, history, and cognition" in a more general sense. In addition, the book's attention is skewed toward the doctrinal religions, especially Christianity. For balance, the theory ought to be tested against such imagistic religions as animism and shamanism. It would also be interesting to see how the theory weighs up against other doctrinal religions such as Islam, Judaism, and certain forms of Buddhism. As a general paradigm, the modes theory tends toward a binary formulation of religion, and this is something which may disconcert scholars concerned with diversity and difference. This point is addressed by Wiebe in chapter 12, on religion among Upper Palaeolithic hunter-gatherers, which Whitehouse's theory would, problematically, categorize as wholly imagistic. The theory also tends to regard imagistic and doctrinal modes as mutually exclusive. Instances where these modes interplay, and there has been historical transformation as a result, remain problematic. And as Clark suggests, in chapter 8, any refinements of

the theory must attend to other aspects of society such as gender. The editors argue for a "scientific" approach to religion. Whitehouse's theory is held to contribute a causal understanding of religion, rather than a hermeneutic one, and so to replace previous "idiosyncratic" approaches. This seems overtly dismissive of a range of interpretative and qualitative work which has been done recently, among it Shanon's work on the phenomenology of religion, including a paper in the first issue of *Time & Mind*. Whitehouse is interested in the psychological foundations of religion and their origins in human evolutionary development. This is an ambitious project, beside which "idiosyncratic" variation must seem unsystematic, and this may account for his annoyance with it. But however "scientific" the apparatus might appear, the chapters in this book evidence a tension between the generality of the theory and the specificity of the case studies. Furthermore, as Wiebe points out, the theory attends to the transmission of religion but not to its cause; it is weak in dealing with historical transformation or "even religion per se." Whitehouse's own chapter attempts to address many of these concerns; but in my view, this book make the modes theory work too hard, without successfully addressing its binary and generalist nature, the dynamic between imagistic and doctrinal modes, or the complexity of the evidence.

Reference

Whitehouse, H., 1995. *Inside the Cult: Religious Innovation and Transmission in Papua New Guinea.* Oxford: Oxford University Press.

Time and Mind: The Journal of Archaeology, Consciousness and Culture

Volume 2—Issue 3
November 2009
pp. 367–370
DOI:
10.2752/175169609X12464529903335

Book Review

The Goddess and the Bull: Çatalhöyük: An Archaeological Journey to the Dawn of Civilization

Michael Balter

Simon & Schuster, 2004
Hb, 416pp. ISBN 9780743243605

Reviewed by Åsa Berggren

It is not often I pick up a book about archaeology and read it as if it were fiction. But *The Goddess and the Bull* by Michael Balter is that kind of book. It is written in a popular style, presenting the story of the Neolithic mound Çatalhöyük in Turkey, with its densely populated 9,500-year-old settlement and its famous wallpaintings and figurines. Or should I say stories?—because Balter manages to tell not just the story of the research of the site, but also the stories of the people involved and the story of how archaeological theory has developed, as well as the story of the Neolithic in Turkey, all in one book. In theory, I would say he is trying to do too much, but in practice Balter manages to integrate all these stories into one well-written, fascinating tale. Aiming at the general public rather than the archaeological community, the book serves simultaneously as an adventure story, an introduction to a high-profile archaeological project, a biography of several archaeologists, and an introduction to archaeological theory. As a science journalist, Michael Balter has written for *Science Magazine* and has been able to follow the Çatalhöyük project over a period of several years. And he has followed it closely. He has done extensive research, visited the site on many occasions, and recorded many in-depth interviews with participants in the project. As a result he has become very familiar with the project and its people.

Both legendary archaeologists and participants unknown to a broader public are portrayed by Balter, but not everyone in the project is mentioned in the book. I was one of those anonymous excavators of the project, participating during three seasons during the time that Balter followed the project, but I never actually met him. As a former participant I read the book with interest. As a trip down memory lane, it reminded me of the people I met, the good as well as the difficult times, the hard work and the fascinating archaeology of Çatalhöyük. Of course my reading of the book is different than that of others, just because I was there. I couldn't help wondering, when reading the many very personal accounts of the participants: Is this really interesting for the general public? My first reaction was, it isn't, but then again, perhaps it is. Getting to know people's personal motives and thoughts may be seen in the light of the explicitly reflexive methodology of the project. It does seem very fitting that this project gets its biography written. A biography could be like a mirror that adds something to the understanding of the archaeological interpretations made about Çatalhöyük, something which makes our understanding of the site more qualified. It could be like a diary for the whole project.

Now, there are two questions I'd like to ask. Does this biography work? And does the biography add anything to our understanding of the Neolithic life at the site? Well, it is a biography of the site Çatalhöyük, and not of the project conducting the current investigation of it. And, on those terms, it does work as a biography. The whole story is told in chronological order. Balter starts with an account of how the site was discovered

in the late 1950s by James Mellaart and colleagues, and excavated by Mellaart and his team during the 1960s. The site's growing fame is followed, as well as Mellaart's career, since they are intertwined. A special chapter is devoted to "The Dorak affair" even though I didn't get much wiser by reading it. What really happened? Did Mellaart, as he claims, meet a woman who showed him a Bronze Age treasure that he made sketches of and later published? Neither the woman nor the treasure was ever seen again, and questions have been raised concerning the existence of both. Balter takes a middle-ground position, suggesting that the treasure really did exist, at least in part, but that the woman perhaps didn't. This affair was a scandal in its time and together with irregularities at Çatalhöyük, such as reports of stolen artifacts, it caused the Turkish authorities to shut down the excavation by the mid-1960s. Mellaart was thrown out of the country but kept promoting the site's importance by publishing his findings, making it known as the first city and interpreting certain figurines as a mother goddess. Whatever her value as an interpretation, the mother goddess now has her own following and Çatalhöyük has become an important site for goddess worshipers. They have a very strong relationship to the site, building on Mellaart's interpretations. The new project has been criticized by the mother-goddess community for questioning these interpretations and disrespecting their religion; so has Balter's book, something which he describes in the preface to the paperback edition.

The next chapter of the site's story focuses on the renewed excavations at Çatalhöyük that started in the 1990s. Balter explains how Ian Hodder, the founder

of post-processual archaeology, came to
be the one to reopen the investigation
of Çatalhöyük, but also how Hodder's
interest of archaeology started, how he
met his wife Christine Hastorf, and other
personal anecdotes. At the same time
Balter manages to give an insight into the
theoretical developments within archaeology
at Cambridge, debates which led to the post-
processual turn and in the end to Hodder's
decision to implement his theoretical ideas
in practice at an excavation. Together the
personal and theoretical accounts serve
as a background to the new project at
Çatalhöyük and its characteristics.

The rest of the book is dedicated to
the new project, its participants and the
excavations on site. Balter leads the reader
through the planning and setting up of the
project, including the achievement of getting
permission from the Turkish authorities and
finding sponsors to fund the project. He
takes us through the experiences of the
first small group to settle in and the first
season of surface scraping, to the following
seasons when the project grew in size and
finally more than a hundred people were
involved on site. He also describes the
reflexive methods that are put into practice
at Çatalhöyük (for which see Hodder 1997).
Descriptions of methods and research
issues concerning the local Neolithic
are interrupted by personal accounts of
several team members. It works, since each
personal story acts as a background to an
issue presented, but something about these
personal accounts bothers me. I think it
has to do with the style they are written
in. Balter describes people's inner feelings
and thoughts in a fictional style, which
paradoxically puts them at a distance.

The story unfolds and Balter provides
accounts of the project season by season,
describing the work on site as well as
developments in interpretation of the
Neolithic. All aspects are covered but
he makes a special point of following the
faunal team, as animals are crucial to some
of the most important research questions
of the project, such as the domestication
of cattle. He also touches on some of the
controversies that arose at the site between
excavators and specialists, a conflict that had
many causes, and escalated during the 1996
season. It concerned the close work of the
two groups, meant to promote feedback and
integration, as part of the reflexive approach
of the project. For various reasons different
goals and agendas came into conflict.
Instead of empowering the excavators, the
reflexive approach left them feeling more like
providers of information for the specialists
than anything else. The problems were
soon recognized and measures were taken
to solve them in 1996. That was two years
before I first came to Çatalhöyük, and even
though most of the problems were solved,
the divide between excavators and specialists
still existed in 1998. I've just reread my
first diary entries from that season where I
mention how I found this problematic. (All
diaries may be accessed on the website of
the project: http://www.catalhoyuk.com/).

Not all issues that are important to the
project are followed up in the book—for
example the multivocality that is stressed
in the reflexive approach. Of course he
gives the researchers a background that is
rarely found in archaeological literature, but
the local group of people involved in the
project is not represented with the same
commitment. To really get into the head

of one of the local men that worked at the site I can recommend a book written by Sadrettin Dural (2007) that complements both Balter's popular book and the academic writings about the site in a very interesting way. It is the voice of "the other" in this context, if there ever was one.

There are many more issues discussed in the book, I have only touched upon a few here. One more question remains to be answered. Does this biography of Çatalhöyük add anything to the understanding of the archaeological interpretations? Well, perhaps it does, in its own way. But it was not written with this objective, and it is perhaps asking too much of this book. Even though Balter gives the reader a very well-informed insight into an archaeological excavation, he still looks at the interpretation process from the outside. The book is written in a popular style, with some exaggerations and dramaturgical turns, which give the archaeological work at Çatalhöyük an air of

exciting adventures and childhood dreams come true – something that I think is wrong. Our job is not a hobby to us. Balter does not mean to belittle our work, but his fascination with archaeology, archaeologists, and Çatalhöyük tends to bias his story, and make it seem like fiction. Taking this into account, I recommend it to anyone, archaeologist or not, that needs an introduction to Çatalhöyük, or anyone that wants to look behind the scenes at a large archaeological excavation, or anyone that needs a break from academic literature, or anyone that simply wants a good read.

References

Dural, Sadrettin, 2007. *Protecting Çatalhöyük: Memoir of an Archaeological Site Guard*. Walnut Creek: Left Coast Press.

Hodder, Ian, 1997. "'Always Momentary, Fluid and Flexible': Towards a Reflexive Excavation Methodology', *Antiquity* 71: 691–700.

**Time and Mind:
The Journal of
Archaeology,
Consciousness
and Culture**

Volume 2—Issue 3
November 2009
pp. 371–374

DOI:
10.2752/175169609X12464529903533

Book Review

Therapeutic Landscapes

Allison Williams, ed.

Ashgate (Geographies of Health Series), 2007
Hb, 373pp. ISBN: 9780754670995

Reviewed by Timothy Darvill

It is widely recognized that certain kinds of landscape seem to promote health and well-being in a positive way, and for this reason may be sought out and promoted. One only has to think of the lure of the seaside for health-giving recreation and respite, and the fact that resorts such as Weymouth, Bournemouth, Brighton, and Blackpool built their reputations as places for rest, recuperation, and convalescence long before the bucket-and-spade holidaymakers arrived in the later twentieth century. The rugged uplands of Britain's National Parks have this role as well. Established in the 1950s as much for quiet enjoyment and recreation as for conservation, they occasionally incorporated powerful places such as Buxton in the Peak District whose health-giving spas had already been patronized for centuries. Gardens are also important, and here one recalls that Vincent Van Gogh painted his famous "Iris" series after roaming the gardens of the Asylum of Saint Paul de Mausole at Saint-Rémy in the spring of 1889, later that year noting that "for one's health it is necessary to work in the garden and see the flowers growing" (Van Gogh 1889).

Studying and understanding the therapeutic role of these landscapes, whether actual or perceived, has developed into a lively academic discipline involving geographers, anthropologists, sociologists, and health-care workers. It emerged in the early 1990s as a branch of medical geography, pioneered by Wil Gesler at the Department of Geography at the University of North Carolina at Chapel Hill. Gesler examined the role of Epidauros in Greece, Bath in England, and Lourdes in France as places with lasting reputations for healing. As Williams explains in her very useful historical introduction to *Therapeutic Landscapes*, the theoretical underpinnings of these studies lie in cultural ecology, structuralism, and the humanities, but as the subject has grown there is increasing attention to sociocultural dimensions of health and the recognition that the healing powers of a landscape depend on its context and are affected by local social and economic conditions and their associated changes.

Therapeutic Landscapes extends the scope of the subject in new and exciting ways, although the word "landscape" may cause confusion in the minds of some readers as it is applied here in a very general way, and at many different scales. Thus for example Collins and Kearns in Chapter 2 examine beaches in New Zealand, Hallman in Chapter 9 explores zoological gardens, Crooks and Evans in Chapter 11 look at the micro-space of the hospital waiting room, while Conradson in Chapter 3 examines the cognitive landscapes of workplace, homespace, and "elsewhere." Most seem to follow the phenomenologically constituted distinction between "space" as one of society's key dimensions that can be physical or imagined, and "place" as a location in space where we find interactions and where experience defines values and dependent realities (as proposed in Tuan 1977).

The twenty chapters forming the core of the book are arranged in five even-sized sections, each offering insights from quite different perspectives. The first deals with traditional landscapes, both natural and built, including beaches; places of stillness and retreat; yoga and the globalization of therapeutic landscapes; and the healing landscapes of the Alps. This last chapter by the book's editor explores the symbolism of the Swiss Alps in Johanna Spyri's well-known children's classic *Heidi*, first published in 1880. The story is of an orphaned girl who lived out her childhood high in the Alps with her grandparents before being taken to Frankfurt by her aunt where she becomes unwell and yearns for her rustic mountain home. Upon being sent back to the uplands she quickly recovers, and similar, almost miraculous healing is also experienced by friends from Frankfurt when they too visit the mountains. With abundant tensions between rural and urban lifestyles, insights on physical, emotional, and spiritual health, and the subtext of trying to live in harmony with the environment, the story of Heidi provides a route through which to explore many of the themes developed in the book as a whole.

Section two focuses on therapeutic geographies and how they affect special populations, including the treatment of substance abuse; clients of the United Kingdom National Phobics Society; European city dwellers; and family-friendly zoological parks. These chapters are followed through in Section 3 which looks at applications in health-care sites—hospital design; hospital waiting rooms; assisted living residences in the United States; and end-of-life homecare. In all cases these contributions show how general thinking about issues of healthcare and the experienced "landscape" have very practical applications.

Section four examines how contested landscapes function in the therapeutic context, including gay bathhouses in Toronto, Canada, where risky sexual behavior jeopardizes the health-giving benefits; gendered used of space in an agrarian Guatemalan municipality; the risks and fears of being in woodlands otherwise considered therapeutic; and Stalinist Gulags and healthy/

unhealthy places. In these contributions the subjective experiences of therapeutic landscapes come to the fore to illustrate how both positive and negative reactions are usually culturally defined, gender-specific, and often contingent on social, political, and economic contexts.

The final section looks at applications in the anthropology of health, including a study of how an asylum landscape was transformed into a residential development in Northern Michigan, based on the new-urbanism movement; care-giving in nursing homes; the creation of roadside art and memorials in the Nevada Desert represented as rock graffiti, stone markers, and cairns; and the role of the aesthetic represented through sculpture, architecture, and abstract artwork in UK hospitals. Throughout these contributions the focus of attention shifts to the complex social relations that develop between participants in health-care, considering the relationship between the landscape and the human body, and asking how landscapes might be relevant to those who do not share the beliefs and assumptions inherent to Western biomedicine.

Pervading all the relatively short contributions brought together in this volume is a strong sense of excitement at the possibilities that these new insights offer, and the practical applications that can be developed. The energy that these researchers have brought to their work is palpable, and their enthusiasm must be admired. Good health and well-being are of such interest to people across the ages and across the world that it is rather surprising that studies of this kind are so recent. And as this book freely acknowledges, there is much more to be done. Except in the final

section and chapter 4 on Yogic landscapes, a strong Western Gaze pervades these papers; other perspectives and approaches deserve greater space and their inclusion would further extend the multidisciplinary and multi-vocal framework which is already a recognizable strength of the discipline. There is also perhaps room to continue Gesler's interest in the historical dimension of health-restoring places whose operation extends back into ancient times. Why do these places survive in the modern landscape? Can they be rejuvenated? And how do the beliefs and traditions attached to them form and get perpetuated? Similarly, it would no doubt be possible to include studies of heritage sites as therapeutic landscapes alongside the kind of places reported here. However, the really big issue, highlighted here but not explored in detail, is the relationship between physical health, emotional well-being, and the socially constructed world in which we live. *Therapeutic Landscapes* starts that debate, and while not all the discussions may seem immediately appealing to readers of *Time & Mind*, this is a book whose real value lies in opening up issues, broadening perspectives, introducing themes for further study, and bringing together experts in a wide range of fields who have something new and interesting to say about the most enduring and fundamental human concern: our own health and well-being.

References

Tuan, Yi-Fu, 1977. *Space and Place: The Perspective of Experience*. Minneapolis, MN: University of Minnesota Press.

Van Gogh, V., 1889. Correspondence quoted in the J. Paul Getty Museum exhibition "Vincent's Irises" 1999. Los Angeles: John Paul Getty Museum.

Time and Mind: The Journal of Archaeology, Consciousness and Culture

Volume 2—Issue 3
November 2009
pp. 375–378

DOI:
10.2752/175169609X12464529903579

Book Review

Sacred Gardens and Landscapes: Ritual and Agency

Michael Conan (ed.)

Dumbarton Oaks Research Library and Collection and
Spacemaker Press, 2007
Pb, 314 pp. ISBN 9780884023050

Reviewed by Bob Trubshaw

Rituals require organized physical spaces, just as they organize
conceptual spaces. What happens if historians with a detailed
knowledge of a broad range of non-Western past societies
start investigating where those societies held their rituals? Will
this reveal insights into how those societies thought about
the landscapes where the rituals took place? *Sacred Gardens
and Landscapes* provides a diversity of answers. Insights
range from cosmogonic myths that situate settlements in
mythic "central places" to the way that formal courtyards
and gardens are constructed to facilitate annual cycles of
formal rituals—just as would be expected if "landscapes" and
"mindscapes" are both the prerequisites and the outcomes of
rites.

The contributions to this volume encompass a wide span
of places and times, among them Classical Greece; Heian and
medieval Japan; Mexica cultures; the Krishna groves created in
sixteenth-century India; contemporary rituals in Sri Lanka and
their roots; Suriname Maroons; Italian ritual horse races and a
purportedly "devotional landscape" created in Norfolk in the
mid-twentieth century. By juxtaposing such a wide variety of
cultures and different scholastic approaches this book offers
a thought-provoking antidote to Western "cognicentrism," if
only by illustrating the wide range of purposes for enacting
rites and the variety of places, spaces, and landscapes where
they are performed.

Landscape is key to most of these chapters. Despite
the title, gardens—or even concepts which approximate to

Western notions of gardens—are discussed by only a few authors, and even then historical records of the rituals enacted in these "gardens" dominate the discussions. Apart from tentative acknowledgement that gardens can be ritual spaces, there is little here to inspire a makeover. The prevailing themes of this book are landscape and ritual.

Each reader will respond differently to the diversity of contributions. Ideas which inspired me include María Elena Bernal-García's discussion of Mexica culture (revealing the specific ways in which cities and their sacred spaces are cosmogonic) and Behula Shah's detailed descriptions of the pilgrimage groves created near Braj in the sixteenth century to manifest Krishna's seduction of Radha, showing how ritual perambulation brings together devotion, poetic literature, landscape, and the erotic.

At a more fundamental level, there are clues as to how cognicentric the Western concept of "sacred" is. For example, neither Classical Greek nor Sanskrit has a word which equates to the modern sense of "sacred." Instead these languages differentiate the *extent* to which places or people are sacred, or distinguish modalities of sacredness (such as "pure, good, auspicious" instances in contrast to "transcendent and timeless" ones). Hindu culture also emphasizes that the sacred is something which is experienced— and therefore part of the process of experiencing the landscape—rather than an innate essence. These are nuances which Western uses of the word "sacred" indiscriminately bundle together, but which need to be considered when discussing the sacred in non-Western societies.

Indeed, there are more things in traditional cosmologies than are usually

dreamt of in Western discourse. *Sacred Gardens and Landscapes* does not simply reiterate that insight but instead repeatedly offers detailed examples of how cultures which are geographically and temporally separate from the West have a wider range of concepts of the sacred and spatial cosmologies than Western thinking normally encompasses. Crucially, as Sarah Bonnemaison begins to explore, rituals are essentially processes by which meaning is constructed and reconstructed, where cosmologies are dismembered and then remembered. By extension, the meaning and significance of sacred spaces and landscapes are created and maintained by the ritual activities taking place there. Meaning is not simply "out there" in a culture but instead continually evolves—although without repetition and reenactment it would be largely forgotten. That most certainly applies to the most fundamental meanings that make up a society's cosmological myths and associated rites. Ritual makes these meanings manifest, as well as providing the occasion to simultaneously transmit the practice and its ideology.

All the contributions are based on documentary evidence of rituals—usually written but predominately visual in the case of the Mexica—so there is no speculation as to how rituals and places acted as "landscapes" and "mindscapes" in prehistoric societies. Neither, because this is a volume drawn together from specific studies, is there an overview of how widely the concept of "sacred" can stretch when removed from the confines of Western discourse. So, although individual chapters are sufficiently self-contained, the overall book leaves open many doors to further thinking.

Such further thinking could verge on out-and-out speculation about prehistoric counterparts. As the Neolithic complex at Avebury has never been far from my thoughts for over a year, I cannot resist disorderly thoughts along the lines of "What if Neolithic people who built Silbury Hill thought, like the Mexica, that sacred mounds were 'earth wombs' from which shamans set off on supernatural journeys?" or "Did the Neolithic people have the same sense of the erotic when perambulating the Avebury 'cycle' as the Krishna devotees at Braj?" It may not have been the intention of the contributors to encourage such wanton conjecturing but for me it is a strength that a book such as this, which can so easily amount to little more than its component specialisms, stimulates more generalized speculation.

There is much here to widen specific and general awareness of past landscapes, rituals, cosmologies, and the nuanced non-Western concepts of the sacred. My only reservation is that the way the book is designed—with exceptionally long lines of small text—makes reading unduly difficult. Academic writing is demanding enough without the task being made all but impossible because the person putting the book together was not aware of the basics of book design. The inclusion of a comprehensive index, however, is to be commended.

Time and Mind:
The Journal of
Archaeology,
Consciousness
and Culture

Volume 2—Issue 3
November 2009
pp. 379–380

DOI:
10.2752/175169609X12464529903335

Book Review

English Holy Wells:
A Sourcebook

Jeremy Harte

Heart of Albion, 2008
Pb, 168 pp plus CD (536pp in total) ISBN 9781905646104

Reviewed by Bruce Osborne

Directly one reads the subtitle it is immediately apparent
by the pun that Harte's sense of humor is going to lift this
mammoth tome from a barely digestible detailed academic
diatribe on an obscure subject into something that entertains
as well as informs the reader. This is a book that comes
in three volumes. Volumes two and three are a detailed
gazetteer of English holy wells, one which is the most
comprehensive ever put together for publishing. Volume one
is a discussion on the origins of holy wells, providing a critique
of theories expounded by earlier scholars and proposing
eighteen different scenarios that have led to the creation of
holy wells in England. Volume one comes with numerous
black and white illustrations within the text.

As Harte indicates in the introduction, one has to
appreciate that there are many different types of holy well
and any effort to collectively assign them to a common
origin suffers from "a radical foreshortening of the historical
perspective." The analogy of "sacred stones" is cited, arguing
that one can similarly not indiscriminately jumble war
memorials, megaliths, tombstones, crosses, obelisks, and
altars into the same box. It is also pointed out that, unlike
many religious edifices, holy wells are merely water sources
and often are bereft of architecture, relying instead on
documentary evidence to establish their provenance. As
is later shown in the text the surviving literature can be
misleading to say the least, often as a result of embellishment
of the legend over time for a variety of reasons.

The value of English Holy Wells as an authoritative
publication is threefold. First, it is a gazetteer of sources and

their recording over the centuries and as such is a prime reference point for anyone wishing to locate and conduct further research on particular sites. The bibliography, in particular, gives students of holy wells a substantial guide to the source material. Secondly, the book's distribution analysis gives clarity to regional variations and origins, although in spite of the substantial database of over 900 sites, subsamples are inevitably in danger of falling below statistical levels to a point where significance is indicative rather than totally reliable. Thirdly, this publication debunks many theories that have been postulated over time about holy wells, both the individual sites and the general category, and as such sets a new standard and framework for scholarly research into the subject.

With a personal interest in Great Malvern, I find it interesting to note how Harte weaves the critical points from many years of historical research into his overall hypothesis. As such it is apparent that *English Holy Wells* is not a stand-alone work of historical research. What we have is an accumulation of building blocks from countless authors and historians over the centuries consolidated into a single work of immense size and significance. As such it is able to draw conclusions on a macro level. For the fine detail of specific sites the scholar then needs to refer back to the source material. Clues are given as to relevant recent local research findings and, in the case of Malvern, the provenance of St. Ann's Well as a name is comparatively recent with a possible much earlier association with St. Werstan, the martyr founding saint of the religious cell. Such a clue gives direction to students seeking more detail.

For the computer-oriented, volumes two and three are summarized on a CD that comes bound within volume one. The CD also contains the spreadsheet that summarizes site characteristics. As such this publication is an essential reference guide for all serious enthusiasts of holy wells. It is also an ideal starting point for local research appertaining to specific sites. This makes it invaluable to the local historian, who can then consider the local scenario in the context of the overall holy-well cult.

TIME & MIND
Notes for Contributors

Manuscript Submissions

The Editors welcome submissions that explore issues related to the areas described in the *Time & Mind* journal description document. Indeed, any relevant aspect of time and mind will be considered as long as *both* those elements form the core of the submission. It is requested that plain language be aspired to, with the use of jargon or specialized terminology kept to the absolute minimum. (Where specialized terms are unavoidable, please supply a glossary.) All submissions considered for publication will be subject to peer review.

Submissions aimed at being major articles should be approximately 3,000–10,000 words in length and *must* include a brief (two- or three-sentence) biography of the author(s), an abstract (up to about 200 words) and up to five keywords. Shorter papers ("Notes") should range between 500 and 2,500 words in length. Interviews should not exceed 15 pages (about 4,000 words) and do not require an author biography. Exhibition and book reviews are normally 500–2,000 words in length.

Electronic submissions (preferred, certainly in the first instance) should be sent to timeandmind@berg publishers.com. Microsoft Word is the preferred word-processing program, where possible. Scanned illustrations will suffice, though originals may possibly be requested in certain circumstances if the submission is successful. (Originals will be returned.) Please scan to letter or A4 size at 300 dpi for photographs/halftone, or 600 dpi for maps or illustrations containing text. Illustrations embedded in Word documents cannot be used. Similarly, graphics downloaded from webpages are not of sufficient quality for print reproduction.

A disk as well as a hardcopy of any finally accepted contributions may occasionally be requested. (Please mark clearly on the disk what word-processing program has been used. Berg accepts most programs with the exception of Clarisworks.) Manuscripts or disks should be submitted to the current *Time & Mind* postal address: T&M, PO Box 11, Moreton-in-Marsh, GL56 0ZF, UK.

Submissions will be acknowledged by the managing editors, and those accepted for further consideration will be entered into the review process. Electronic manuscripts and scanned illustrations will not be returned. Submission to the journal will be taken to imply that the article is not being considered elsewhere for publication, and that if accepted for publication it will not be published elsewhere, in the same form, in any language, without the consent of the editors and publisher. It is a condition of acceptance by the editors of a submission for publication that the publishers, Berg, automatically acquire the copyright of the published article throughout the world. *Time & Mind* does not pay authors for their submissions nor does it provide retyping, drawing, or mounting of illustrations.

Style

The journal's text will use US spelling and mechanicals. *The Chicago Manual of Style* [15th Edition] is our style guideline, and *Webster's Dictionary* is our arbiter of spelling. While it would be preferred if contributors used US English, submissions in British English will be acceptable (though such submissions will be transliterated into US spelling and mechanicals). We encourage the use of major subheadings and, where appropriate, second-level subheadings. Manuscripts (whether electronic or hardcopy) submitted for consideration as articles must contain: a title page with the full title of the article, the author name(s), address and affiliation where relevant (do not place the author name(s) on any other page of the manuscript), a two- or three-sentence biography for each author, and a 200-word abstract. Up to five keywords are requested to aid in any future library searches. Please present the keywords after the abstract.

Electronic manuscripts can be either single- or double-spaced. If hardcopy manuscripts are involved, then they must be typed double-spaced (including quotations, notes, and references cited), one side only, with at least one-inch margins on standard paper using a typeface no smaller than 12-point. Authors should retain a copy for their records.

It would be preferred that submissions be presented with paragraph breaks involving a line space (double line space if presenting a double-spaced text, of course) between paragraphs and without first-line indentation, as in this set of guidelines.

Notes and References

References to *notes* are to be by means of consecutive numbers inserted in-text throughout the paper and are to be written up at the end of the text. (Do not use any footnoting or end-noting programs that your software may offer as this text becomes irretrievably lost at the typesetting stage.)

For *references*, the "Harvard system" is to be used in-text, thus:

> Centuries ago in Europe, country people were terrified of the walking dead, of "revenants" (Smith 1989). They developed all kinds of protective procedures (Jones 1957; Morris 1972, 1984), and though these may seem bizarre to us now they were deemed absolutely necessary at the time.

The cited references should be presented at the end of the paper, after any notes, in this manner:

References

Dewdney, S., 1962. *Indian Rock Paintings of the Great Lakes.* Toronto: University of Toronto Press.

Dowson, T., 1992. *Rock Engravings of Southern Africa.* Johannesburg: Witwatersrand University Press.

Fagg, B., 1957. "Rock Gongs and Slides." *Man* 57: 30–2.

Goldhahn, J., 2002. "Roaring Rocks: An Audio-Visual Perspective on Hunter-Gatherer Engravings in Northern Sweden and Scandinavia." *Norwegian Archaeological Review* 35(1): 29–61.

Hedges, K., 1990. "Petroglyphs in Menifee Valley." *Rock Art Papers* 7: 75–82.

Lawson, G., Scarre, C., Cross, I. and Hills, C., 1998. "Mounds, Megaliths, Music and Mind: Some Thoughts on the Acoustical Properties and Purposes of Archaeological Spaces." *Archaeological Review from Cambridge* 15(1): 11–34.

Palmer, D. and Pettitt, P., 2001. "In Search of our Musical Roots." *Focus* 105: 80–4.

Rajnovich, G., 1994. *Reading Rock Art: Interpreting the Indian Rock Paintings of the Canadian Shield.* Toronto: Natural Heritage/Natural History Inc.

Reznikoff, I., 1995. "On the Sound Dimension of Prehistoric Painted Caves and Rocks," in E. Taratsi (ed.), *Musical Signification.* Berlin: Mouton de Gruyter.

Rowland, I. and Howe, T.N. (eds.), 1999. *Vitruvius: Ten Books on Architecture.* Cambridge: Cambridge University Press.

Offprints

On publication, authors will be sent a PDF eprint (with nonprinting watermark) of the final, published version of their article for personal use, and will be able to order a free copy of the issue in which their article appears.

5th biennial
University of Bristol and Time & Mind

ROCK-ART SYMPOSIUM

This year's theme will be

Underlying Mechanisms

Speakers will include:
**Christopher Chippindale,
Aron Mazel, Angelo Fossati,
Jamie Hampson
and Paul Devereux**

The Symposium will take place at the
University of Bristol, 43 Woodland Road, Bristol
on Saturday 24th April 2010
10am to 5pm

Tickets £20
For further details contact Dr. George Nash on
George.Nash@bristol.ac.uk